THE GLOBAL NOMAD CLUB

A NARRATIVE ANTHOLOGY

NATALIE LEA BERTSCH

GLOBAL NOMAD PUBLISHERS

ISBN: 978-3-9525262-3-1 (hardcover copy)

ISBN: 978-3-9525262-4-8 (paperback copy)

ISBN: 978-3-9525262-2-4 (ebook copy)

For my Global Nomad family—you know who you are.

ACKNOWLEDGMENTS

I love the acknowledgements sections in books. They are like a secret story to grasp: how the book has come to be, and who helped writing it. Sayuri, you are the embodiment of the global nomad I had in mind when writing the book—gifted, curious and full of questions.

A very special thanks to the contributing authors who collaborated with me on this book: Pooya Ghoddousi, Scott Burroughs, Jepkemoi, Gabriela Blatter, Stefan Bigler, Ruben Barreto, Maciej Bugala, Andrea Roberts, Candy Estolatan, Beth Cabagon and Myra Ferrer. You are talented and brave to share your stories.

I would also like to thank Priscilla Koukoui, Chad Hamre, Meriaty Subroto, Megan Shea, Jason Lu, Simon Schmid, Janine Walz, Ana-Maria Torres, Claire Macquard, Kim Thomond, Samantha Booth, Cédric Crelo, Emil Bolongaita, Katherine Guy, Marion Tessier, Tito Santos, Suchin Teoh and Taric de Villers for agreeing to be interviewed and for inspiration.

Special thanks also to Chhandak Pradhan and Ariel Margalith, for going above and beyond, as well as Tatjana Lanaras, Joel Wong, Lidia Zabala, Sylwia Orczykowska and Rajshree Saraf, for helping me create unique visuals for the crowdfunding campaign. And Sylwia, aka Little Lady Funk, again, for creating this beautiful cover.

I want to thank all of you supporting the crowdfunding campaign. Profound thanks goes to the *Global Nomad Publishers,* who are mentioned in the *About the Author* section.

Anima Slangen—thank you. You are not only a dear friend but also the best editor I could imagine; and this while you were moving half around the globe. Without you, no doubt, this book would not exist.

Ariel Margalith—you are a wonderful friend and true creative. Thank you for all the advice on the book and especially the visuals. Also, thank you for Incredible India – for getting lost together and finding delicate beauty.

Pooya Ghoddousi—thank you for the friendship and that critical mind of yours. The book is better for it.

Florina—thank you for being my favorite sister. You were there when I was not on firm ground, and if I walk calmly today, it is also because of you. Shahbano and Vale—thank you for being there during a very special time of writing this book.

Maurice—thank you for your light and happy heart; it translates into unwavering love for us. And finally, Timéo Georges—I am grateful for your sweet nature, and those large blue eyes. You gave me depth.

PROLOGUE

"The universe is made of stories, not atoms."

— Muriel Rukeyser

Rapid advances in technology have fused the world of the 21st century into a dense web of global connections. The process of globalization is simultaneously creative and destructive, transforming the bond of humans with the physical space they inhabit, redefining the affiliation between citizens, cities and the nation-state, and blurring the lines between the known and the other.

Inequality across countries has decreased dramatically since the beginning of the millennium, with large emerging market countries turned into global economic powerhouses, shaping the emergence of a multi-nodal global economic system. Old and emerging global cities compete with nation-states for talent, resources and influence, and have become destinations for voluntary transient migrants, or global nomads as they will be referred to in this book henceforth. They move for a variety of reasons, including dysfunctional politics, work opportunities and relationships. Their arrival provokes mixed emotions from local residents, ranging from heartfelt embrace to open rejection. And with the ability to attract people, knowledge and investment, (global) cities reposition themselves against the nation-state. At the same time, citizens with various degrees of freedom to exit gain greater independence from their home countries, shifting the power balance between them and the state. Ultimately, urban structures, and the formal and informal rules governing them, emulate the socio-economic changes and adapt to the weight of the newly arrived. Gentrification, alien restaurants and a multitude of foreign languages on the subway tell a tale of change.

Global nomads and local residents alike have used the internet to connect in virtual space beyond the physical borders of countries and cities. More than a mere medium of exchange of ideas and images, a "like" on social media promises the possibility of true connection, but also breeds the ground for division. The images of Aylan Kurdi, the drowned migrant boy washed ashore in Turkey, and George Flyod, the Afro-American murdered by the police, bound people around the globe in outrage and cause—if for a moment. In contrast, internet bots have been used to spread misinformation with the objective to exacerbate domestic political divisions and influence elections. Social media has contributed to fragment the diversity of political and social discourse by globally connecting people with a set of similar beliefs and values in virtual echo chambers. Global nomads have used the internet to create global communities of like-minded people, an informal loose nation of many—growing, overlapping, reversible—leaving footprints in physical and virtual space. We see a multitude of fragmented but connected global stories.

At the intersection of the socio-economic transformation of contemporary societies and the globalization of human lives, global nomads have permeated the social fabric of urban spaces. By choosing to move from one temporary urban residence to another, they explore alternative nomadic narratives, challenging the dominance of human experience in sedentary habitat. At this crossroad, we meet Leya, a 20-something claiming identity, happiness and belonging throughout her global journey which, as a Spanish native, she is privileged to navigate with few obstacles to her mobility. Her trajectory touches and overlaps with other global nomads', and yet is starkly different from other migrants' with fewer choices than her.

In Chapter 1 (Identity), Leya lives as an exchange student in Bangkok and shares her adventures with her sister through email. Eventually, she creates *The Global Nomad Club*, a blog through which she explores the globalization of identity, love and urban spaces. The blog connects her with a physically dispersed community of fellow global nomads, transcending and expanding her own experience. The chapter deals with belonging and the identification as global nomad, as well as racism in this context.

In chapter 2 (Love Interrupted), Leya explores the particularities of international romances. She enjoys the endless opportunities and new encounters, but also experiences the added layers of complexity in relations transcending national identities and physical borders. Her blog reflects her personal development through several short stories about love and relationships in a global setting.

In Chapter 3 (Glo-cal Relations), she moves to Beijing, where she integrates into a more local life. Her blog entries analyze the possibility that global nomads may contribute to social fragmentation in their cities of residence. Do local citizens and global nomads merely share physical space, or do they truly engage with one another?

In Chapter 4 (Weight), Leya returns home to Barcelona. After graduating, she moves to San Francisco, where her blog becomes increasingly reflective on the wider social impact of her lifestyle choice. What weight do transient residents carry in their host country? How do they affect political systems in their home countries (e.g. by voting with their feet)? In this last chapter, Leya becomes a voice for her fellow global nomads while finding answers to her questions, which compels her to start the blog in the first place. The chapter talks about gentrification, civil rights, democracy, citizenship and the refugee crisis.

While growing up and wrestling with the identity she chose for herself, Leya's understanding deepens with the diverse multitude of people she encounters throughout her journey. Their stories challenge her to see the world through another set of eyes and to realize the differences in personal narratives. Globalization needs a kinder angle—one in which these multiplied global connections lead to a deeper understanding and more profound acceptance of the other.

Whereas Leya is a fictional character, the short stories and essays on her blog are inspired by places I experienced, and are also crowdsourced from real life global nomads. I am grateful to all the people who opened up and contributed to make this book an authentic attempt to portray and critically reflect on the global nomad experience. My hope is that the questions and stories raised here are much larger than Leya's journey and will reach and resonate with you, wherever in the world you are.

1

IDENTITY

*C*rossing *oceans and skyscrapers. Left but not arrived. Flying. Falling. Rising. New beginnings. On the move. Darling, where are you going to?*

From: Leya.Nunez@gmail.com
To: Patricia.Nunez@gmail.com
Date: 26 November 2008. 17.20 (Bangkok time)
Re: my birthday party

Darling sister, I know this letter is long overdue. Bangkok is just too much. You really should come visit. I miss you! Are you sure you want to know what is going on in your little sister's life? It's Sunday afternoon and I just went to bed a few hours ago, the first time since getting up on Friday morning. I went out with friends from the exchange program. I guess this was my birthday gift to myself (happy 23rd birthday to me!). I only wish I remembered more of this night. I do remember, however, that the police raided the club, and everyone had to take a drug test in front of live cameras. I can only blame my clouded memory on too many vodka red bulls and of course, champagne, courtesy of the French crowd.

I can't call you now because I'll be leaving for a study group in a little while. I know you wonder, but I think it was the right decision to come to Thammasat University, despite everything that happened. I am having so much fun. I hardly miss Barcelona, with the exception of you, obviously. The other night I dreamt I was walking over a very long bridge. I started running faster and faster, but I just could not reach the end. My eye caught a glimmer of silver from the reflection of the water below and when I looked down, I felt I could finally stop running, just like that. It's a good sign. You can all stop worrying, especially Maman and Abuela. I will write them and let them know how the midterms go. One of my professors has been encouraging me to consider public service. I don't know, I've always seen myself as a future business executive. Did I mention that I selected software engineering as a minor? And I do have to think about my upcoming practice semester required for graduation. Too many questions for a day like this one. Kisses, Leya

From: Leya.Nunez@gmail.com
To: Patricia.Nunez@gmail.com
Date: 1 January 2009. 22:59 (Bangkok time)
Re: global nomad

My dearest Patri, I am wishing you a very happy new year from Bangkok. After enjoying myself last night, I had a quiet lazy day, reading a very interesting piece on contemporary nomadism. My friend Amory gave it to me some time ago. It made me think about who I am today, and about who I want to become in the future. Maybe today this is who I am—a global nomad? Was it a conscious choice or just mere coincidence that I have come here? Kisses&hugs, L.

Nomadism: Glimpses (reprint)

— Pooya Ghoddousi

They are nomads. They move around, rear animals. For centuries they have pitched their tents throughout the year under the sky, the sun, the rain.

In a country composed mainly of arid and semi-arid terrain, the nomads migrate with their livestock to make use of the scattered resources, a technique acquired through refining the hunter-gatherer lifestyle. By taming animals, they could carry their livelihood and their household with them, so their journeys became cyclical and their return trips planned.

Their peoples are organized: tribes, sub-tribes, clans, etc., with a name for each. Each of them knows their place in the tribal hierarchy, allowing them to be recognized by fellow tribesmen. You might call them free, wandering without restraints, but these ties can be quite restrictive, a strong set of traditions and unbreakable social codes devised to ensure their survival.

Lately their way is changing – their lifestyle, once adjusted to the rhythm of nature, is being eroded. Their livelihood, full of hardships but once the most productive of the land, can no longer compete with the demands of the market economy. Their children receiving modern education want to become doctors and engineers. Lured by the bright lights, many have yielded to sedentarization forces, changed their way of life, become settled and semi-settled, even to become [urban] parasites[1]. During the past century these forces have reduced their numbers from one third of the overall population to less than two percent today. Today, they are trying to survive.

The tent is their home, their flexible, mobile home. An architectural masterpiece perfected through the test of time. Its fabric and shape adapt to the seasons, the weather and the size of their families. The tent is a shelter to them, their animals and their future. The finest layer of fabric between them and the sky, the frailest shelter to recreate a universe. Tents are habitations that spring up spontaneously, creating homes in the blink of an eye. Tents as havens of security, as a warning to the outside world that a limit cannot be trespassed. Tents as ephemeral human presence, strokes on the landscape, drawn then erased. They pitch them not too close, not too far from each other. They need the air, they need the space. They are their only homes within the open rangelands, vast areas once their territory being trimmed down today. The settled life keeps expanding, urbanization keeps moving toward them. Cement buildings are replacing their woven tents. They are nomads still trying to be.

He is a nomad. An urban nomad. He lives in a city. City or urban sprawl, settlement gone out of control? He is new to this place, like so many other millions. In a short while the village has become a metropolis. An overgrown head to a malnourished body. In this country, a third of the population is under 30. He has experienced revolution, war and bombardment. He leads a double life—in the public and private spheres—in this ugly, overpopulated, polluted city. He has learned to adapt to the situations and enjoy life. He has even developed a liking for the dynamic and colorful spirit of the city. Anyway, isn't it a mirror of the heterogeneous mix of people, characters and identities of which he is part?

Unlike his peers, he doesn't hate the place, although sometimes he does feel that he has had enough of it – the traffic, the pollution, the frenzy of people, style. He came to life in this melting pot after his parents moved here. His family, friends and the people he grew up with constitute his 'tribe'. This tribe defines his identity for the most part, regardless of geography, territory, states contained by boundaries. This is his nomadism. His home here is temporary. It houses only a small piece of his heart. During his childhood he had to get used to the pain of losing them one by one when they left Iran for better prospects abroad. At any moment, he might also leave to join them.

Most of the new buildings that have mushroomed in the city appear empty. Real-estate speculators have bought so many of these city apartments and are now just waiting to sell at a better price. The feeling of it is of people in transit, humanity passing through.

He is an urban nomad. He lives in a city. He works for it, sleeps beside it, makes it grow. He is a construction worker. He pitches his tent on open urban spaces. Is he reclaiming a bit of freedom amidst the inferno of stone and steel? No, probably not. His tent is only a very far-removed sister of the nomads' tent, a tool necessary to his work. Is he a nomad? He does move from site to site, and his belongings are few. He lives on the ground, far away from the apartment heights he helps to build. He does not migrate with the seasons, he is not part of an environmentally sustainable lifestyle. He is an ad-hoc, mobile appendage to a system that yearns for sedentarism with eyes teary of the freedom it is giving up. His city is a nomad too, somehow. An unsettled settlement.

His city is millions of concrete tents huddled close together, looking for space, searching for fresh air. Civilization here has put aside the rules of nature, and the symbiosis it should adopt always and however large its settlement becomes. Nature reminds us sometimes.

He is a nomad. An earthquake made him so. He is a Bami, his city razed by 90% by an earthquake measuring 6.6 on the Richter scale. Forty thousand of his fellow citizens were taken away, and the historical clay citadel, a monument of world heritage protected by UNESCO and their major tourist attraction, destroyed. The houses which once lined avenues, streets and alleys have changed into tents distributed by humanitarian agencies and pitched on the dirt. Only the date palms remain standing. The people of Bam have been brought the closest possible to the ground. For thousands of them, the temporary housing of the tent has become a home and has brought into being a most precarious style of life. Their tents are a fine line between desperation and hope.

She is a nomad. A global nomad. She is not a tourist, not an immigrant, not a refugee. She has been on the move before she came to know herself, first following her parents and then in search of something missing...Experience? Belonging? Identity? Happiness? She cannot say where her home is; perhaps a few places are home to her at the same time.

As a child she didn't like being dragged from place to place, but now that she looks back she cannot think of it in another way. She lives in a shifting present tense, not being able to predict or plan much further ahead. She sometimes thinks that if she wants to start a family, have a child, etc., she'd better hurry. But even that is not a must; too many options and no clear road map.

She is one of the growing numbers of people in the world who cross borders in search of a better life[2]. She left the motherland. Like her ancestors, what is vital for her sustenance is dispersed in different areas, causing her to migrate frequently. Driven by opportunism, she grazes in one place before moving on, forced to go or lured by a more attractive prospect. Nor can she abandon her birthplace altogether. She needs that space, she needs that air. She is the 21st century nomad, the e-nomad of the post-industrial era. She hops from place to place, keeping in touch through different means of communication: email, e-communities, phones. Perhaps her home is where her friends, relatives, co-workers are, relationships she creates wherever she goes. Her environments are heterogeneous mixes of different people and cultures. She is eclectic and herself a piece of a multicolor collage.[3]

From: Leya.Nunez@gmail.com
To: Patricia.Nunez@gmail.com
Date: 11 March 2009. 11.43 (Bangkok time)
Re: boys

Hello, dear sister. Figures! There are new boys. Let's start with Aaron. I met him at a café here in Bangkok (or BKK as everyone calls it here). He was talking loudly with his friends about his tattoos. I eavesdropped on their conversation then started chatting with him. We talked the entire afternoon. He explained to me every tattoo on his arms. There were a lot. As we were talking, he would text with one hand while running his other hand through his thin brown shoulder-length hair. I even caught him using the iPhone mirror app a few times to check himself out, his tight red-checkered shirt, his carefully undone hair. Anyways, he was fun. He invited me to his apartment and I stayed.

Also, remember the German guy working for Mercedes-Benz? Max. He's always in BKK for a few weeks at a time. I'm not sure what he does, exactly. Not because he couldn't explain it to me but because I simply lack the patience to listen. Anyway, I found out he is married! Seriously, who hides their wedding ring in the bathroom?! Every time he's in town, he asks me to come to his hotel. The other night he gave me this whole speech about how I need to get my life in order and that partying is not a substitute for a life plan. And did I want to stay in Asia forever? And how I would never get married if I continued living like this! After this little speech, I decided I was done with him.

And then of course there is Etienne, the Frenchman. We call him the poet. All we do is talk and talk about the state of the world. Worrisome according to him, full of opportunity if you ask me. Well, worrisome and full of opportunities. We talk about books, mostly the ones he's read. I am busy enough catching up with class readings in between alcohol-fueled nights and early mornings. I don't know what he wants from me. So far, we only talked. L.

From: Leya.Nunez@gmail.com
To: Patricia.Nunez@gmail.com
Date: 12 April 2009. 23.11 (Bangkok time)
Re: Tattoo

Patri, Aaron is inspiring me to get a tattoo. He sent me this short story recently printed in the city magazine he is working for, and I attached it for you. I am thinking about a tiny sparrow below the wrist. What do you think? L.

— Scott Burroughs

There's nothing on my arm right now. Well, nothing other than arm hair and a few freckles, of course. I plan on changing that with a tattoo. I've been planning to for a few years now, but I decided to put it off until I turn 30. That's in a year and a half. I figure that if I'm not certain about it now, maybe I'll be wise enough to make a decision then.

I'm also putting it off because my family is against it, but once I'm 30, they will have no choice but to relinquish their moral lease on my body. To me, getting a tattoo is a massive decision. A permanent one, the type I'm beginning to realize I'm deathly afraid of.

I'm trying to figure out why I want to get one and where the idea even came from. Maybe it came to me at an airport waiting lounge or riding one of the infinitely long escalators of the St. Petersburg metro. Maybe it came in a vodka-induced dream. But somewhere in the gray-white grips of the Russian winter, I think I realized that I was becoming a completely different person than I was born to be and that I needed to somehow commemorate the metamorphosis.

See, I'm not from Russia. I'm not Russian. I'm a white boy from what was once a little speck of farmland called Middletown in the easily forgotten state of Delaware, which for those that never got the extra credit question in geography class is on the East Coast of the United States. It's a fact that I have to regurgitate to almost every person I meet, because I haven't even lived on the East Coast for about 10 years. And in that time, I haven't lived anywhere for more than 3 years at a time.

When you change cities and countries so often, you change so much more than just addresses. You change your perspective and values. I'm not religious, but for me, every plane ticket is like a communion wafer. It washes away all your sins and concerns. It lets you start fresh. I just worry some of the good things get washed away as well.

So, I want something that can't be washed away. I want to etch in my arm the names of all the cities that I've lived in and that have changed how I define myself. Already when I think about my life in Taipei for instance, I can't remember the name of the town that I would ride out to for a swim. And when I think of my life in Rome, I can't remember the name of the piazza where I waltzed with a complete stranger. I fear that as I get older and live in more cities and collect more memories, I might even forget some places altogether.

But if I have my memories on my sleeve, I'll never forget. The places will always be with me, and I can even share a little piece with anyone who gets close to me. Imagine, when I'm 50, I can look at the little Shanghai above my elbow and think, 20 years ago I thought I knew it all. Then I'll revisit Mardi Gras a second time when I look at the NOLA on my bicep. The joys of playing in the woods as a little boy will rush back into me as I look at the DE close to my heart. I'll slip right back to the skyscraper rooftop clubs of Taiwan when I see Taipei on my forearm. The Roma on my triceps will bring the taste of prosciutto e melone to my tongue.

Maybe it's not a good idea, but it's my idea, and for now it seems like one of the few things that really belongs to me. In that washing that happens at 40,000 feet, I've probably lost a lot of the good things. And certainly by leaving—always leaving—I've passed up a lot of really great things. But this little regret is never enough to root me down. I don't know if I'll ever settle down. The old blues guys say "Wherever you lay your hat is your home." For me, I guess it will be "Wherever I tattoo is my home." I don't really wear hats.

From: Leya.Nunez@gmail.com
To: Patricia.Nunez@gmail.com
Date: 16 April 2009. 23.11 (Bangkok time)
Re: Chinatown

Oh, Patri, on bad days, I head over to this street lined with fish restaurants in Chinatown and eat at a stall owned by a man named Khun Somchai. His face is weathered like the seaman he used to be. He moved to Bangkok when he got married and now has a seven-year-old son. He doesn't like to talk much and is usually busy serving clients steaming hot fish with ginger, lemongrass and chilies. I like to sit at his stall, eat fish and think. When he is free in between customers, he sits with me and we exchange a few words. Mostly about the weather (always hot). If he is feeling talkative, he will talk about his son and the things he wants to teach him. To always look out for yourself because otherwise someone will take advantage of you. Or sometimes he praises him when he does well in school. I wonder if he is happy. He never complains but rarely smiles.

Meena, a woman I keep randomly meeting at Khun Somchai's, always teases me about my visits, saying Khun Somchai must think I'm very lonely, although I constantly assure him that my tears are from the chilies he so generously provides. Meena recently retired after working most of her life as an international civil servant in Asia. She spends

one third of the year in Manila when her native Netherlands
is too cold. We meet at Khun Somchai's when she travels
through BKK on the way to Manila and other places (she
often stays a few days at a time to visit old friends in the
city). Sometimes it feels as though we compete for Khun
Somchai's attention. You think he could have shared a boat
with our father? I remember father before he left us—so full
of life, always smiling and singing softly to himself. Maybe
Khun Somchai was changed by the sea, made into a
thoughtful man of few words I've learned to appreciate. Do
you think I will still be traveling when I am Meena's age? L.

From: Leya.Nunez@gmail.com
To: Patricia.Nunez@gmail.com
Date: 3 May 2009. 23.11 (Bangkok time)
Re: Abuela

Patri, tell me. How is Abuela? I thought about her today
after reading a letter from a grandmother to her granddaughter, which I found in a book left behind in a restaurant
on Kao San Road. I loved it and copied it for you. Would you
please read it and tell me if you like it, too? Please send
Abuela my love. I miss you all. Kiss, L.

My dear granddaughter

— Natalie Bertsch

I look outside waiting for your light, quick footsteps
approaching the house, ready no doubt to tell me your latest
adventures. And I feel the time has come to tell you my
story. The story of how this house has become a home and
refuge from a life full of instability and new beginnings. I
wonder if my parents, Katia Hall and Ernst Bach—you

never met them—could have imagined how their lives, and in turn mine, would unfold. My mother grew up in Jaffa (part of today's Tel Aviv)—daughter to hotelier Moritz Hall and lady-in-waiting to the Ethiopian Empress, Katarina Hall.

> "Moritz Hall married Wälättä Iyäsus, also called Katarina (or Katherine), on 17 May 1863. At the time of their marriage, she was fourteen years old. Her mother was Assete Worq Maqado, a member of the Ethiopian aristocracy, the first Ethiopian wife of the German Christoph Eduard Zander. Emperor Tewodros, whom Moritz Hall worked for, began to drink in excess and became vindictive. He now imprisoned all the English missionaries, including Moritz Hall and his family... On 13 April, Easter Monday, 1868, all the captives at Mäqdäla were freed by the British military expedition led by General Robert Napier, sent to rescue the British prisoners. During the battle and the storming of the fortress, the Emperor Tewodros took his own life."[4] My grandparents and the other liberated foreigners left Ethiopia along with the British forces. They were offered a passage to India with the returning British troops of the Indian army, but they appear to have traveled to Syria, perhaps to Baghdad. Refugees in search of a home, they arrived in Jaffa in 1874 and settled in the neighborhood known as the "German Colony".

> — TOBY BERGER HOLTZ

My parents met during the First World War in Jaffa, where he served as member of the German army. How they fell in love? I wish I could tell you, but I do not really know. After the war ended, they left Jaffa for Jüteburg in Germany, where my father, a pharmacist and convinced pacifist refusing to bear arms, worked registering leftover medications of the war. I was born in 1919. Two years later, my father received the offer to run his own pharmacy in Berlin. Our growing family—Hans and I become brother and sister to Gitta and Hella—followed suit.

In 1923, we relocated to Neutempelhof in Berlin. I feel there is where everything changed. After five years of relative quietness, your great-grandfather left us to live with his lover, an acquaintance of the family. I am not sure if you can imagine how unusual this was in the 1920s. His decision sent me on a whirlwind journey to different places and boarding schools.

To avoid scandal, I was immediately sent to boarding school in Oberschlesien. Only one year later my sisters and I moved to another boarding school in Braunschweig, where our mother taught English and French, which she spoke fluently because of her upbringing in Palestine.

A few months later, I received the news that my father had died. That he was fatally shot by his lover, who—after killing him—took her own life, I only learned many years later. We believe he wanted to return to the family, but sadly never made it. I turned 12 years old that year, and while still grieving, our concerns had become existential. With him gone, I had lost most financial support, and then the boarding school in Braunschweig was closed because of financial difficulties during the great depression. We were sent to another boarding school in Hermans-Werder, while our mother remained in Braunschweig to guard the closed school property for a small salary.

Eventually, my mother ran out of money. Your great-grandfather did not leave any pension since as a pharmacist he had been self-employed. We lived off my mother's meagre salary as a teacher—and now guardian of the closed school property—and the proceeds from a life insurance claim. Initially, the insurance company had refused to pay on grounds of suspected suicide. My mother proved it to be murder by demonstrating that my father's body's temperature was lower than his lover's at the time of death, ruling out suicide.

The difficult financial situation forced me to skip class in boarding school. Since level 10 students were allowed to smoke, I took up this bad habit when I was only 14. And look at me now, still enjoying a cigarette while writing this letter to you. In 1936, new laws under the elected Hitler regime prohibited the teaching by non-academics such as my mother. Our financial situation became unbearable and my mother decided it was time to leave Germany for good. Since our family had lived in Ethiopia and served the Imperial Court in different capacities for generations, it was arranged for her to teach at a local school in Addis Ababa.

Once again, we packed all our belongings and travelled to Hamburg to wait for the necessary paperwork for our journey to Ethiopia. Among others, we required a declaration of good health for my skin illness, which still pains me unless I visit my mother's place of birth and take extended baths in the Dead Sea. When we finally received all the clearances required, realpolitik ended our hope of a better life in Addis Ababa. Italy attacked Ethiopia in 1935, forcing my family to leave the country. Our relatives in Addis Ababa sent a telegram that under no circumstances should we return to Ethiopia.

The telegram contained, however, a second line advising us to go to where the Apostle Paulus taught his wisdom—

Cyprus. We travelled all across Europe to Brindisi on the sole of the Italian boot. From there, we spent one week on a boat to Cyprus. I remembered being terribly seasick as violent autumn thunders stirred up the Mediterranean Sea.

Nanny, as my mother was called by everyone, transferred a thousand pounds to Barclay Bank in Nikosia, as requested by Cyprus law, in order for us to set foot onto the island. We moved into a little pension called *Fair at Home*, owned by a friend of the family. My mother continued to teach English and French, while I started vocational school.

When it had just turned spring, I received an unexpected offer. The German Consul in Jerusalem asked me to take care of his children and attend university in my free time. For a displaced half-orphaned girl at that time, this was an offer of a lifetime. Politics did however upend my life once more. Just turned 18, I had to return to Germany to serve my so-called fatherland duty.

From Mediterranean Cyprus, I was sent to the north of Germany near Finsterwalde in Brandenburg in 1938. Hard field work and milking cows became my daily work routine. I do remember the meals consisting of nothing more than bland potatoes and salt. There was not much spare food in a country preparing for a devastating war. Germany eventually became responsible for starting the Second World War, which killed 60 million soldiers and civilians, including the Holocaust on 6 million Jews.

In 1939, I finished fatherland duty and reattempted to leave for Jerusalem, when the German administration denied my exit because of the upcoming war. Separated from my family, I moved in with my uncle Josef Hall, who lived in Stuttgart. Well-connected, he found a job for me with the oil company Shell. I remember-feeling unhappy in the house since he was not used to young adults and was therefore overly strict. Interestingly enough, the decision to work for Shell would change my life in unexpected ways.

I had to take phone calls from clients as part of my secretarial duties. Born in the north of Germany, I did not understand the strong dialect of my clients from the rural South. A young colleague helped translate it, and it turned out to be the beginning of a life together. He was very open-minded compared to my other work colleagues, who mistrusted my darker skin, which I have inherited from the Ethiopian side of the family.

He was very good-looking and immediately attracted my attention. It was all quite exciting, really. I admit, I was quite unexperienced with men, given my oriental education and exclusive attendance of girls' boarding schools. With summer giving way to fall, he had planned a big party—possibly our engagement party—at his family's house in the vineyards surrounding Stuttgart. Unfortunately, it never took place, because he was drafted to serve and was sent to Poland on the 1st September 1939. He left without even being able to leave me a note.

Although your grandfather served on the eastern battlefields of the Second World War, we regularly wrote to each other. In 1943, we got married in a small ceremony at the family house in Stuttgart. While we were on the train to our honeymoon, a letter calling your grandfather back to the warfront was already making its way to us. He immediately returned to the field.

For a very long time, I did not have any news from him. I was worried sick, especially since by this time I was already pregnant with your uncle. And then, in 1944, I moved to live with a close friend in Meso near Finsterwalde (Brandenburg). After losing all the soldiers of his unit to snow and bullets, your grandfather—wounded himself—was finally sent home from Leningrad. His wound, a grazed shot in the upper arm and not life threatening, was a blessing in disguise. I will always remember him playing tennis, with the scars of the bullet still visible on his upper arm. Fortunately, he received my telegram asking him not to return to Stuttgart but go to Finsterwalde instead.

Around 1945, the Allied Forces had inflicted substantial losses to the Germans and the Russians had advanced to 15 km from Meso. Hitler prohibited the civil population to move in order to prevent the enemy's advance. Yet your grandfather, as a commanding officer, was ordered back to Stuttgart. His status in the army gave him the right to be accompanied by a nurse. He assigned me as his nurse, providing me with the necessary papers to leave Meso. That is how I escaped the approaching Russian soldiers, and most likely sexual assault, which so many women experienced during the liberation of the world from Nazi Germany.

With the permission papers to leave, I took the train to Schorndorf, a small city near Stuttgart. All in all, I had to change trains 13 times. At one train station, completely exhausted, I left all my belongings on the track and eventually asked a soldier for help. "Where are you going?" I asked. "To Stuttgart," he answered. In a last effort, I clenched his belt in my hand and followed him, holding your uncle really tight with my other arm. When we got on the train, I remember seeing a mother giving birth on the platform. The images of this trip forever imprinted my memory, and maybe because of them, I remained in touch with this soldier through my entire life. Meanwhile, your grandfather deserted the army to flee the arriving French.

Eventually Germany surrendered on 7 May 1945. Having deserted the army, your grandfather had to hide in our flat. It was only after the establishment of the US administration in 1946 that he was able to receive new identity papers to reenter civilian life and work. In 1948, your father was born. In the very same year, we built our house in Stuttgart. This house would finally become my home and put an end to the nomadic life I so deeply despised.

I see you roaming the world with your long blond hair, carefree and appreciated in your difference. My own experience has been so very different in this regard. And with all the questions you asked about my life, I never told you how painful moving places was to me in my youth. Constantly considered the new and exotic girl, with my darker skin and black eyes, I found this traumatizing. I have memories of moving to Berlin, where a neighbor boy welcomed me with a slap in the face and called me a stupid Jewish pig. What a cruel boy, you would say, but indeed that was the way my morning had started that day. Back then, we were forced to hide our oriental descent to obtain the Aryan proof as a question of survival. On one of my first days in a new school, I sat next to a girl who ran home crying and told her mother about the new dirty girl in class. She told me this many years after we had become close friends. And then again, she did not need to tell me because in my heart I already knew. And until this day, I still have access to all of it, the words that stung like a sharp needle, the mistrusting looks that deeply hurt me, and the sound of that slap. Today, everyone thinks how interresting my life story is. But at the time, the reaction of people was very different.

I agree with you, darling granddaughter, the world has become a different place since my school days, but racism remains the ugly reality of our globalized world today. I watch images of refugees arriving in their new home countries on the news. I only see their scared, hopeful looks, and my heart reaches out to them. I wish they could avoid the hurtful racism I experienced, but when I see the violence and hatred their arrival often provokes, I have little hope. Each and every one of them comes with a unique story worth listening to. I hope you will. With all my love, Lilo

From: Leya.Nunez@gmail.com
To: Patricia.Nunez@gmail.com
Date: 20 May 2009. 02.31 (Bangkok time)
Re:

Hi to my favorite sister! I've started limiting myself to two drinks a night. Turning point was a few nights ago. Some of us did shots at *Bed Supperclub*. Anyway, when the club closed at 1 a.m., everyone was still in the mood to party, dance and swim. So, we decided to go to a friend's house. It was this massive apartment somewhere on Sukhumvit Road, with an endless number of rooms. We went to the kitchen and had one more drink. I don't remember what happened next. I just woke up in my dorm on campus. Saaki had put me in some bright pink university shirt. She took my hand and asked if I remembered what had happened at the apartment, but I did not. She'd found me on some guy's lap, making out. When she asked if I was OK, I apparently insisted I was fine. But minutes later, the guy and I were gone. She frantically opened every room until she found me passed out on a gold-painted bed under bright chandelier lights. He was standing above me while I was comatose. She yelled at him and threatened to break every bone in his body if he didn't leave me alone, and then took me home. I managed a half-smile and made silly jokes about men in general, but the truth is I'm so shaken by this experience, the violence of what did not happen. I always felt I was living my life the way I wanted to. Free to choose, free to be a powerful person (once I put my mind to what I actually wanted to become powerful in), free to be like any man. But what did not happen reminded me how we are still not equal. As a girl, you can never allow yourself to lose control, not even for a second. Unsafe until kept safe. Eatable. Digestible without my mind. What is the taste of my silent body? Does it taste like metal? My eyes closed and my head turned away. Tell me. It must be sickeningly dull. How dare you? I remember him more clearly now—a foreign government official attending a conference in Bangkok. Suddenly I feel sick. I wish I could erase the thought of men like him.

Anyway, I don't want to worry you. I know you have your hands full with Abuela. Has the latest health scare made her softer, I often wonder? I think more of home. I should help you. Come home, just like she would want me to. But Asia still calls out to me, Patri. I want to prove myself here. Prove I can make it here and be successful. After Saaki told me what happened, I went straight to eat at Khun Somchai's. He must have felt I was sad, because he put extra chilies in my food so I had an excuse to cry silently. That same night, I wrote down thoughts for my first blog entry. I have named my blog *The Global Nomad Club* and am writing as lil_sea_girl. Watch out for my first post in the coming days. Love you so much, L.

The Global Nomad Club
25 May 2009

Hey, restless hearts out there, lil_sea_girl here. This is my first blog post. I will not lie to you, these last days have been difficult. Bangkok has taken me utterly by surprise, conquered my heart and soul, and then spit me out feeling overwhelmed and alone. This is why I am reaching out to you, fellow global nomads. You might have just arrived in the city—still lost in translation—or about to leave to your next destination. I am planning to publish short stories, interviews, and poems about our strange and beautiful global life. I also want to hear from you. Please do tell me, what keeps you up at night? Do we share the same questions?

Good night, fellow nomad stars! Yours, lil_sea_girl.

From: Leya.Nunez@gmail.com
To: Patricia.Nunez@gmail.com
Date: 1 June 2009. 7.23 (Bangkok time)
Re: blog

Dear Patri, did you read my first blog entry? I gained a few followers and received one message, which encourages me to continue. But as you requested on your last email, I need to tell you more about my friends. Obviously, there is Saaki. She takes language classes at Thammasat University. We immediately hit it off when we met in Thai class. She travels in between two jobs and recently left New York, where she worked as a hairstylist for years. We have a lot in common, such as our family situation, and we do wonder how our lives will unfold. There are a few Spanish girls in the exchange program. We obviously have an easy connection and commiserate with one another about the lack of choices for Spanish food in Bangkok. But in my view, they complain too much. It is too hot, it's too humid. Really? They did not realize that Thailand is a tropical country when they signed up for it? The classes are too difficult. No, they are too easy. The guys are only interested in Thai girls. Oh, get over yourself. Of course, I don't say these things and just nod sympathetically and look for either Saaki or Amory to escape from their conversations. I finally got to tell you about Amory, my favorite guy here. How he is from the US and extremely smart. How he is always one step ahead of me. How he knows everyone and is always invited to the right parties. But he is also an old soul, extremely observant and always challenging me to better understand myself. Together we cry over boys. Me (mostly) about the general absence of a boyfriend and he about a Thai aristocrat he is in love with. Yours more than ever, L.

The Global Nomad Club
Urban Nomad: A Brand in Motion
13 June 2009

Hey there, restless hearts, I am back with a new piece on entrepreneur Jepkemoi. We talk about multi-faceted identities, fashion & jewelry, and the power of the internet to create decentralized peer-to-peer supply chains.

Jepkemoi is an entrepreneur who just recently moved to Manila with her husband. We met while she was on vacation here in Bangkok. We have a common passion for jewelry and fashion, and have shared several discussions on global entrepreneurship, style, business models, urbanism, belonging and the inability to truly belong anywhere.

— Jepkemoi

Just before starting my graduate studies a few years ago, I founded my brand called Urban Nomad, creating handbags from leather and canvas. I worked with local women groups in parts of the production to help increase their income and skills. The brand's main concept was to transform traditional and indigenous African fashion and jewelry into pieces that were attractive and accessible in global contexts such as New York or London while still maintaining a strong Kenyan identity. A distinct Kenyan story.

I stopped the work during my graduate studies in London and restarted the brand under a different name and with a new concept when moving to Manila. Sole Living stands for Sustainable Organic Local Ethical business practices. The name is a work in progress, and it reflects me evolving as a person. It represents the choices I believe in, the choice to consume consciously and to keep in mind the impact our consumption has on the environment. That is why I support and buy from smaller designers lacking global market access. While the designers I curate have global appeal, they lack the platform to showcase their designs to a global audience. Sole Living wants to bridge that gap by connecting local designers with global markets and at the same time providing consumers with the opportunity to consciously support ethical products from smaller designers featuring outstanding contemporary designs deeply rooted in the traditions of their respective locale.

How did I go from being a designer to curating the work of other designers? A part of me wanted to keep the handbag business. I realized as a designer, I had to promote my name.

However, I found it more challenging and interesting to promote other designers. Also, to speak frankly, there is so much mediocre s**t out there. Until I feel inspired enough to do amazing stuff and until my vision is an utterly compelling narrative and encompasses all aspects of myself, my own creative process will remain a work in progress. Sole Living will focus on being a platform for other designers to showcase their brand.

The name Urban Nomad just came to me, and it somehow beautifully reflected how I felt—where I don't seem to fit in a specific place while at the same time and to a certain extent fit in everywhere. I move from one city to another like a nomad and never truly know where my home is. In some ways, I have made peace with the idea of never finding a home but am content with the certainty that I can carve a space everywhere I go.

Given my half-Kenyan, half-Jamaican heritage, I never truly felt accepted growing up until I met a group of really interesting girls in university who all had international backgrounds. It was only when one of them told me she felt completely defined as a global citizen that my idea of self started to form, of how the differences in my upbringing made me different and how they always would. I suppose it was only then that my sense of identity started to add up. It's still a work in progress. I love and feel totally comfortable in cities like London and Paris where there is a constant flux of people moving in and out from everywhere in the world. They are urban nomads, like me. For now, Kenya is my home and heart but there will always remain in me a longing, a search for the perfect fit.

Moving to Asia has played a critical part in changing my thinking about consumption and the role that we each must play. While the manufacturing capacity of Asian countries is impressive, I remain overwhelmed by the sheer quantity of low quality, substandard and homogenous products that seem to be created all over the continent. Products that lack any form of creativity, artistry or beauty. This for me is particularly sad as there is so much beauty in local culture, techniques and craft. Who is going to buy all this stuff that is being created? I imagine it ending up in landfills and oceans, destroying the planet.

I want to be part of the growing movement aiming to change the conversation on responsible consumption. In developing countries, wealthy consumers tend to follow a pattern of being overly concerned with their status and using western brands and high-end designers as means to advertise it. It's a story flashing separation based on affordability and access rather than what fashion should be—an expression of personality and creativity. Part of changing this focus on status is to showcase the beauty and diversity of smaller, global designers.

While I live in Manila, my target market is the expat community. I hope that by not only showcasing international but also Filipino designers, Filipinos themselves will start to take pride in what is being created in their own country by their own designers. As part of my business strategy, it is essential to understand the culture and sensitivities of my customers. At the moment, Filipino customers seem very focused on well-established mid-range to high-end designer fashion. This might be a shallow generalization; I also notice that their taste seems to slowly be changing. But for now, the business I am building targets global citizens (who may or may not be Asian). I am trying to tap into their common preferences and similar tastes.

One significant challenge that I face is that essential information on registering and starting a business is often hidden or spread across different information sites without any clear guidance. This includes the rules on foreign ownership in the Philippines. It is tempting therefore to register the business in a place like Hong Kong, where the ease of doing business is much better. I think one of the ways that governments and business associations can improve on the numerous challenges that entrepreneurs face is to have regular boot camps with easily accessible information, dedicated "desks" for those interested in starting a business. It would also be worthwhile to think about an association for global entrepreneurs without any specific national attachment to share ideas and best practices.

I would love to create a beautifully curated online platform that is the definitive source for up-and-coming designers from developing countries. One challenge is that I love the idea of having an internet shop on paper, but I do miss actually physically meeting and interacting with customers. Internet shopping gives you the convenience of having a "mobile" shop, so to speak. However, it prevents true interaction and dialogue between the customer and the product. How does that make me feel? I don't want to lose the social aspect of shopping, which includes being with friends, laughing, relaxing and getting inspired. One of the remaining challenges for me is how to replicate this experience in the e-commerce space.

I hope you enjoyed the piece. Thanks to tunappe31 and joynomad77 for checking in with me. I do feel much better since my last blog post, and meeting people like Jepkemoi make me think about how I will claim my belonging and home. I am half-Spanish half-Filipina, and I have felt completely at home in Spain. Maybe because I do look more European than Asian, others never questioned my identity. But being in Asia has made me realize that I too have a more complex identity. Sometimes it feels like people need to simplify multi-facetted identities by assembling them into boxes and finding a fitting label. We should do better—let each other live and try to leave theses boxes unchecked.

Sleep tight, fellow nomad stars! Yours, lil_sea_girl.

2

LOVE INTERRUPTED

olding you. Just never long enough - a plane always meant to leave. Running back to you. How could you let me go? Will I still kiss you next year in spring? Dreams of feeling whole in tiny time bubbles. A collection of happy squares. S.c.a.t.t.e.r.e.d.a.c.r.o.s.s.m.y.w.o.r.l.d.

From: Leya.Nunez@gmail.com
To: Patricia.Nunez@gmail.com
Date: 20 July 2009, 21.27 (Bangkok time)
Re: mushrooms!

Patri darling, Last weekend we travelled to Koh Chang, a beautiful Thai island. I needed a break from Bangkok to chill, and the beaches of Koh Chang were the perfect place for an escape. We were drinking at a restaurant one night when these guys from the bar offered us magic mushrooms. Given my recent encounter with the near unconsciousness, I asked Saaki to share one with me. We promised each other we would stay together. We ordered dinner and for the longest time I did not feel anything but the metallic taste of mushrooms in my mouth.

After dinner, Saaki and I lay down at the beach part of the bar, waiting for the mushrooms to kick in, and restarted our discussion. The one we always have. We wonder about love and if we will find someone living life the way we do. The conversation goes as it usually does until, suddenly, reality blurs with hallucination and my friends Sri and Toto join our discussion. I've told you about them—they're the couple I met in Rome two years ago during my summer internship. They impressed me by combining their careers while at the same time living together (unlike so many other global nomad couples). Anyway, I'm lying down talking to Saaki and I hallucinate that Sri and Toto are actually with us, telling me how they took turns at compromising their career for the other. They tried to tell me something else, but I was not sure I was ready for their message. I tried to block them out of my thoughts. I mean, they were not real! "Listen," Sri replied. "Just be open and ready to compromise and you'll find someone sharing a life and career abroad." I turned around and suddenly heard Abuela's voice. "Come home, otherwise you will never find a good husband. You'll end up like your mother, marrying a foreigner, a creature from the sea, not made from the same cloth you are cut." It was too much. "All of you, please just leave me in peace. I am only 23 years old. Can't you see that?"

I think I yelled out loud for real. I don't know what else I said but Saaki seemed hurt by my outburst and told me how she thought I was spoiled and self-absorbed and did not realize how easy life came to me. I snapped back at her. Doesn't she see that my life is a mess? Later everything became very fuzzy, but I definitely remember seeing two mythical creatures, half-bird, half-turtle, cruising over the perfectly silent sea into a purple-lilac sky. I wanted to stay there, away from everyone talking about me and judging me. Of course, even the mythical birds had to go to sleep at some point. We went to bed early. I woke up the next morning with a splitting headache and Saaki still exchanging as few words as she could with me. When we arrived at the Koh Chang minivan station, the bus was delayed. It gave me time to apologize and buy Saaki her favorite Thai coffee with two extra sugars. That won me a smile she could not suppress. Many hugs, L.

The Global Nomad Club
Decision Art
25 July 2009

Hey there, restless hearts. I hope life is treating you all kindly. I want to share a short story I received from a reader of the blog. And it is true, I have been contemplating love lately—the absence of it and the difficulty of framing and reframing love within the context of the global life. It is a story about decision-making, and how more choices enrich life, but also make it that much more complicated. Please do send me more of your complicated stories!

Decision Art

Shanghai. July 2005. I thought about the city I had so easily embraced. I admired the senior citizens exercising in Shanghai's numerous parks. Watching their faces, I could only begin to imagine their lives and the stories they witnessed. The country turning republic. The city occupied by foreign powers. The atrocities of the Second World War. Being unified, independent, and communist under Mao Zedong. Famines. The Cultural Revolution. And finally, Deng

Xiaoping opening China to the world and restoring her historical relevance.

A few months earlier Luca joined me in this constantly changing urban space of over 21 million people. After a freezing winter with no central heating and a grey spring, summer finally arrived. With temperatures spiking to 40 degrees Celsius and sweat, pounding humidity, Shanghai transformed into a concrete jungle. The difficult decision to leave the city became a little bit easier and we finally agreed to enroll at the London School of Economics (LSE) for graduate studies.

Just when everything seemed settled, I received a call about my Fulbright scholarship application to Columbia University in New York. Did I still need funding? This unearthed a string of new decisions to be made. I thought about New York vs. London; Columbia University vs. LSE; a US education vs. a European education, extremely vs. moderately expensive tuition fees; and finally, Luca vs. school and my professional future.

22 July 2005. The Fulbright commission asks me for an answer by the following day. It seems such a life-changing decision and a truly contemporary dilemma.

1. How much is love worth?
2. How many persons are destined to become our lovers in a lifetime?
3. Is it you that makes me happy, or is it me?
4. Does love really exist if, as one painfully learns, it may inexplicably fade?
5. Are we unique or always replaceable?
6. How much does happiness count if its memory is spoiled by a lover's betrayal?

7. Do we really love someone more than ourselves? How do we know for sure?

8. Are we rewarded for making the right decisions?

9. Is chance guiding our lives—paying obviously right decisions with bad outcomes and the other way around?

10. What can we offer and what do we expect to receive in return?

11. Are decisions the beauty of life?

12. Do we feel the strength of life, its complexity and contradictions most when faced with decisions?

13. Are we necessarily evolving to decide more wisely?

14. What do lovers do?

23 July 2005. Sleepless dreams and no answers yet to all these questions. A little girl puts a white flower in my hair and suddenly I am surrounded by a group of girls touching my hair with shy laughter and asking where I was from. I am in Nobang, an outside district of Shanghai, at a private school for children of migrant workers. Around 300 million migrant workers rush to the big industrialized cities in China to find work. There, they do the so-called 3D jobs—dirty, dangerous, and difficult. They build the glittery skyline and iconic landmarks of Chinese cities, and work in the numerous restaurants, homes, and factories as waitresses, maids, nannies, and industrial workers. Though the type of work is diverse, their fate is similar. The *hukou,* or household registration system, constrains the mobility of labor in China by attaching all social benefits to the birthplace of each citizen. A migrant worker's status is dictated by his or her respective native city or village, with all social benefits such as children's education and health care attached. In addition, migrant workers are not welcomed by urban residents and are perceived as potential competitors

for resources and jobs. Yet despite these difficulties, life in Shanghai seems to them preferable than where they are coming from.

Children of migrant workers are excluded from public schooling in Shanghai and instead go to private migrant schools such as this one in Nobang. I am visiting the school on the day of the *gaokao*, the Chinese national entry exam. This very competitive exam requires intensive preparation and determines acceptance to a specific university and subject of study. Given the limited financial resources of the school and the low book- and teacher-to-student ratio, most of the kids here will not be able to compete for university spots with Shanghai residents who work with private tutors.

I was standing there, white flower in my hair, and smiling at all these beautiful and smart kids, but my mind was distracted by the need to decide between two world-renowned universities. It felt unreal and unfair to decide in the presence of these kids who probably wouldn't be able to attend university at all. And yet, the need for a decision was real, tormenting my thoughts.

Afternoon and back at the office, I seek advice from my supervisor. He says it is fine to turn down a prestigious scholarship. Somewhere in the conversation he mentions love. The discussion helps to form my decision. I call and decline the scholarship. The disappointment is evident on the other end of the line: the scholarship administrator personally invested time and energy to get me the scholar-ship. I just feel incredibly tired.

Zurich. January 2007. Together with Luca in Zurich after having completed graduate studies, I do not feel like myself without a job in a city where professional success is every-thing. I start regretting my decision to not go to New York. It takes months but I finally receive an interesting job offer and leave for Nairobi, on my own.

Nairobi. 28 May 2007. 6.07pm. Kenya Airways is not yet ready for check-in. Three weeks after my arrival, I received an invitation for an interview. A unique opportunity with an international organization in Bangkok. I immediately booked my flight and departed for the airport. There is a small restaurant at the airport. The waiter seems very nice. And yes, steak sounds good.

6.35 pm. Two pilots eat and quietly enjoy their drinks. Another whiskey is served. I sincerely hope they do not fly my plane later. "Monsieur Jubert de Swiss International Airlines est prie de se rendre au depart" (Mr. Jubert of Swiss International Airlines may immediately go to the gate).

6.39pm. A woman and two military men enter the establishment. They each have a Coke and talk intimately. One of them greets an older official in uniform sitting in the back. Grey hair—he exudes serene calm. I wonder what he does for a living. Maybe he is a pilot. "Monsieur Jubert de Swiss International Airlines est prié de se rendre au départ." I am so nervous my stomach turns. The light is too bright, swallowing my thoughts and time.

6.52pm. "Kenya Airways passengers, please proceed to check-in." More patience is needed, but the revelations that follow are a sufficient distraction; the grey-haired gentleman turns out to be a senior official at the check-in counter. Monsieur Jubert, tout le monde vous attend. Famous Monsieur Jubert is in front of me at the fourth passport control station. Only a few more minutes and I will finally take off to Asia.

Bangkok. 11 July 2008. On my first day, I learn that my new employer regularly recruits from the LSE while leaving out many schools in the US. It appears as though prioritizing love has served me professionally, and at the same time, placed me oceans apart from Luca.

Tell me:

1. Is life funny?
2. Was this the right decision? Each different time would bring a different answer to the same question. Every step and decision we make shapes our reality and creates our world as we move along. So, is there really an objective answer to whether or not its counter-factual would have been preferable?
3. Are there parallel universes in which all the different options available to us are actually fulfilled? If so, in such an infinite universe that is expanding ever faster, are other options drifting further and further away from us, reducing our chances to observe the outcomes of alternate decisions made by our other-selves from different cosmic patches? Will technology one day allow us to access our other soul-selves? And would it help desperate decision-seekers?
4. Is decision-seeking a form of art— incomprehensible at times, beautifully complex, and sometimes painful—with ever-unpredictable outcomes from the first stroke of paint?
5. Are global nomads asked to be artists more often?

NOT THE END

P.S.: Parallel Universe

"Scientists now believe there may really be a parallel universe—in fact, there may be an infinite number of parallel universes, and we just happen to live in one of them. These other universes contain space, time, and strange forms of exotic matter. Some of them may even contain you, in a slightly different form. Astonishingly, scientists believe that these parallel universes exist less than one millimeter away from us. In fact, our gravity is just a weak signal out of another universe into ours. It all started when superstring theory, hyperspace, and dark matter made physicists realize that the three dimensions we thought described the universe weren't enough. There are actually 11 dimensions. By the time they had finished they'd come to the conclusion that our universe is just one bubble among an infinite number of membranous bubbles which ripple as they wobble through the eleventh dimension." In every collection of 10 (10122) cosmic patches, we thus expect there to be, on average, one patch that looks just like ours. That is, in every region of space that's roughly 10 (10122) meters across, there should be a cosmic patch that replicates ours—one that contains YOU, the earth, the galaxy, and everything else that inhabits our cosmic horizon... and so every possible action, every choice you have made and every option you've discarded, will be played out in one patch or another".[1]

Sleep well and love bravely, fellow nomad stars! Yours, lil_sea_girl.

From: Leya.Nunez@gmail.com
To: Patricia.Nunez@gmail.com
Date: 29 July 2009. 22:59 (Bangkok time)
Re: more boys

Hey, little sister, I am back to BKK now for a few days, where all my thoughts about the permanence of love and marriage seem out of place. Aaron (tattooed guy, remember?) randomly called me so many months after our encounter at the café. We hung out that night. I like his couch and could forever look at the photographs he took traveling all over Asia. I was feeling warm and slightly numb from all the red wine, so much so that I didn't even mind when he started ranting and obsessing about his colleague from the magazine he recently started working for. It was a blur of wine and meaningless words. I later left and told myself I would never go back. I've met people like him so many times. Enamored with themselves and incapable of seeing others or asking questions about other people. Or maybe it was me who was self-absorbed and quick to judge, taking the moral high ground when I feel I am not really entitled to it either. Maybe I was the one not taking the time to go beyond his rambling. Maybe there would have been more to it. He called my name, but I was already out the door.

This week, I kept my promise to meet with Olarewaju, a banker from London. I forgot why he was in Thailand, but we met at a party last week and he asked me out on a date. He turned out to be the perfect gentleman, gentle, ordering room service for breakfast and having the hotel car bring me back to campus. And he made me think (for a change!). He seemed passionate about his job—talking about his career ambitions, about him wanting to find a wife and have kids and how he would like to contribute to society (maybe by mentoring students from less privileged backgrounds). Deep down, I know there is so much I want to achieve myself. I am conscious of how I waste time partying, and in some ways, I feel relieved the exchange year is coming to an end. I need to take a break from the happy, exhausting, hedonistic home Bangkok has been for me over the last year. On our last date, Olarewaju looked over my application letter and CV. He laughed when I told him that the way he describes his job as a banker makes me want to do something other than finance. He said my CV looked fine, so I sent it out.

There were more dates (none interesting enough to be mentioned in this glorious secret space of ours), but more importantly, I have upcoming finals. Etienne, the poet, asked me to travel with him after we finish. We've decided on Cambodia, Laos and the Philippines. It seems like the perfect post-exam, post-Bangkok plan. But what do I do with him? There is so much palpable tension between us, but he refuses to make a move. I am tired by this tease, but I would also hate to lose another friend if whatever this is does not work out. I called my friend Ana, who is the most positive person I know. I don't know if you remember her— we studied English together in the US before starting college, and remained close. I needed her to tell me that I am doing the right thing and that it will all turn out well. She said I shouldn't worry. I told her about the applications to Taobao, an e-commerce company in China, and Amazon in Seattle, and that if I got accepted to both, I would not be sure which offer to choose. And what to do with this poet? She laughed and told me to trust myself, that I did actually know the answers to all these questions. I am not sure I believe her, but just talking to her made me feel better. XoXo, L.

From: Leya.Nunez@gmail.com
To: Patricia.Nunez@gmail.com
Date: 17 August 2009. 22:59 (Luang Prabang time)
Re: travels

Dear Patri, I am still travelling. First we went to Cambodia, and then to Laos. We've been getting along. He acts as a protective shield against my destructive guy habit. I have to admit, all this travel has been good for me. Images of forests and golden temples have emptied my thoughts. When we were in Laos, the poet and I biked to a temple in Luang Prabang. We spent hours in the temple complex, and it was in this quietness that I realized Ana was right. I did know the answer. I am not done with Asia yet. We cycled back home, and I sent an email to Taobao in Beijing accepting their offer. The days passed quietly. It was so hot and humid that I stopped thinking about the poet's tease since my mind was like floating coconut water.

And then it was time for us to fly to the Philippines, our father's home. He missed it profoundly but never made us visit, as though if he went, he would not find the courage to leave again. And then he died without visiting for a last time. It feels like such a long time ago, Patri. Do you still remember him? Just before boarding my flight to Manila, I swear I felt his presence. I deeply longed for his laugh and the warmth he brought to our lives, I mean before he left Mama and before our house became a silent prison of disappointment and never-ending expectations to fill his place when it was never ours to fill. Remember how we could not feel him there anymore? I look more like Mama than him, and most people do not even realize that I am half-Filipina, so I don't see a trace of him in my face when I look into the mirror. You look more like him—do you still see him? Is it possible that I feel him now in the place where he was happiest—in anticipation of the sea and unconfined by the physical structure of our house? Do you remember him the same way? Was he really happy by the sea, as I remember, or simply unhappy with Maman? Was his work simply an excuse to escape an ordinary family life? You can tell my head is filled with strange thoughts. It happens on the road. Hugs, L.

The Global Nomad Club
LOV
23 August 2009

Dear restless hearts, I am currently traveling through magical Southeast Asia. I feel grateful for the experience and will soon descend to the Philippines, my father's home. Tonight, I want to share a short story written by my friend a_mor_y84. LOV is a threesome love story.

LOV

It was one of these exuberant nights full of random encounters. "So where are you from?" Ophelia did not feel like engaging in one of the pre-scripted where-are-you-from discussions among foreigners. "I was born on a Russian submarine, so I have to get down there once a year to stabilize the pressure in my ears." Vikesh smiled and liked her immediately. They entered the nearby St. Paul's Cathedral after dancing into a new London day. Together they glanced at the chapel's majestic ceiling until it was time for breakfast and post-night talks at a café close by.

Their lucky encounter turned into a carefully coordinated sequence of meetings all over London. Perfect fusion. His smell. Her infectious laugh. Two minds. One thought, really. The Piccadilly line between Covent Garden and Russell Square turns red from the almost daily commute between their places. Two London hopefuls falling in love. He had just started out with the Sadler's Well company, and danced most nights with her in the audience. She'd recently joined a boutique investment firm. The city seemed to love them, and they became part of its boundless inspiration. When July came, Vikesh was scheduled to leave on a worldwide company tour. Amidst dew and fresh tears, they exchange last kisses at the break of dawn. Traffic diverts from the Piccadilly line to fiber-optic cables under the sea.

Vikesh: I think you gave me too much to feel. You moved me profoundly.
Ophelia: Love me now. Love me later. Love me always. You feel so far today. Your world out of reach. And here I am waiting for you and the creation of a new world. A new world the size of a Russian submarine.
Vikesh: I miss you. Your presence is peace. It's light. And I am in such a dark place right now. I hurt my foot and won't be able to perform tonight.
Ophelia: Holding you.
Vikesh: I have seen your picture in the papers. How beautiful you are. I have been replaced until I fully recover. Kisses from Cape Town.
Ophelia: I wake up to the thought of you and carry you until I am exhausted enough to fall asleep at night. London is dreary without you. Work is going well. I will be in Dubai to do a presentation soon.
Vikesh: I can't reach you. The foot still hurts. I need you so badly. In Copenhagen tomorrow.

Ophelia: I lost my flight connection. Sorry, darling! I can't do this anymore. When are you back?
Vikesh: I overheard company staff. They are not sure if my injury will fully heal. Afraid they will not renew my contract.
Ophelia: Come home. You need to see your doctor here in London. Just returned from Dubai. I had an absolutely amazing stay. They offered me a job. Out all weekend. They have a decent ballet company, too...
Vikesh: One week. I can't wait, my darling.
Ophelia: Come home.

After months of separation, he finally stands in front of her apartment. Slightly nervous, he tries to fully picture her face, but some details merely elude him. She takes a second listening to his physical presence on the other side of the door before she finally opens. They awkwardly embrace. There it was. An invisible paper wall made of moments lived apart. But then late into the night, their connection reemerges unscathed and bright. Moonlight talks and quiet happiness turns an apartment in Hunter Street into their only universe. Days and months pass by. Together. Insepa-rable—Vikesh, Ophelia, and the city.

Until one day, an old wound—covered under layers of muscles and her kisses—resurrects itself. Exposed, it burns under the occasional rays of sun bestowed on the city. And the foot does not stop hurting. Suddenly, the grey around him becomes infinite. People's faces lose all expression and become so blank that they don't seem real anymore. Friends feel like acquaintances. Hope becomes a concept—a theory not applicable to him, only to others. To her. She embodies all lost hope. The city, which was his inspiration, whose creative energy had carried him further like riding the top of a wave, seemed to shovel back, overpower and wear him out. How to get off the tube with all these strangers blocking his way? He gets pushed aside and almost misses the station exit.

She watches him helplessly. He is begging her to leave him. To leave him and his broken foot behind. "How can you love me and my tortured soul?" "How could I not?" She can't admit to herself that she is considering leaving. At the same time, she feels attached, guilty, in love. She wants to carry him. But then again, her shoulders seem so small in these shop window reflections on Oxford Street.

The city finally takes a turn against Ophelia, too. Lehman Brothers collapses in the US, spilling over and dragging London along with it. The city morphs into Vikesh's state of mind; or maybe he was just an apostle of darker days ahead. Within weeks, the streets are filled with disoriented people holding square paper boxes brimming over with their office belongings. Shops close. It is a changed city. And then Ophelia becomes one of them. She endlessly evaluates her options. Vikesh. Dubai. She finally decides to break up with London and everything in it. Maybe she'd already decided on the day he nearly missed the tube exit.

She moves to Dubai. Walking to work, her smile carries a faint trace of sadness from their inexplicable loss and, for what it is worth, gives her face the depth it was missing before. But she still can't bring herself to think back to the day she left, when through the silence embracing them, she heard his heart break into a million pieces.

Vikesh slowly picks up his life through the numbness, the physical pain, and the grey. His wound and heart stop hurting. The foot starts healing. His soul recovers. He starts dancing again and rebuilds a life for himself in London, which slowly emerges from the crisis. A quieter life though. Just like the city. More than one year passes and Ophelia returns to London for Christmas. Dubai is still too recent of an adventure for her to feel at home. They meet in one of the pubs, with many friends surrounding them. In a quiet moment he approaches her. *"Didn't we live and lose something so beautiful?"* St. Paul's Cathedral is just a few hundred meters away, white, silent, at the same time beginning and end—eternal keeper of the city's lost, unspoken tales.

Poetic dreams fellow nomad stars. Yours, lil_sea_girl.

From: Leya.Nunez@gmail.com
To: Patricia.Nunez@gmail.com
Date: 27 August 2009. 15:23 (Manila time)
Re: blue

My darling sister, we were only in Manila for a few hours before we flew to Coron on the island of Palawan. Patri, I wish we could have seen papa's home together. I could stay here forever and stare at the sea and her interchanging shades of turquoise and blue. Are colors capable of healing a broken heart? It seems that way. For the first time since it happened, I talked about Xavi. I told the poet how he left me during our first month together in Bangkok, a new city, after being together for so long and jointly planning this exchange program. How it was so difficult for me to understand. I told the poet how Xavi and I met two years ago, during our first year as engineering students at the Universidad Politècnica de Catalunya. How he invited me to his study group. That he was what Abuela secretly wished for me, someone stable, grounded and, most of all, someone from "here" as opposed to someone from "there." That back then he so clearly adored me, and it was me who convinced him to apply for the exchange program. That if it was up to Xavi he would have stayed in Barcelona, close to his family who adore him and the many friends he loved to entertain. I told the poet that I knew Xavi's mother secretly despised me because she thought I was taking her precious son away and that she said so without any words.

The end of us happened so fast. I still can't believe I did not see it coming—that's why it was so painful. We moved to Bangkok, settled in the same student residency, and then, within a month, he left me for another girl from the same exchange program! I remember the week before it happened. I constantly tried to hold him, but our embrace left me feeling empty—he was already gone. I try to remember if there were signs and I simply ignored them. When I initially spoke of the exchange program, he was fervently against it and even asked me to decide between him and the program. I may have convinced him to join, but I also forced a decision, which broke his trust in me.

I still dream of him. In my dreams I try to hold him, but when I touch his skin, he changes form, morphs into granulated brown sugar crumbling to the ground. I try to transform myself, becoming minuscule so I can dance within the delicate structures of his sparkling sugar crystals. But no matter how hard I try and how often I run my head into the wall, my body does not cede, does not change form—not even the smallest bit. We are so disconnected we are not even made from the same elements anymore. And while retreating from each other, we are like charged electrons, violently pulling apart at the speed of mutual disappointment. But when I'm awake, I can't bring myself to see him, talk about him, even mention his name. Saying his name, I fear will make the sky fall and crush my tired bones on the way to class. But the truth is that he has remained under my skin—paper-thin—the entire time. Cutting fast with raging razors at night, inflicting quiet pain while I was at school, with other boys or at Khun Somchai's. Is skin thinner, razors sharper, a heart capable of greater hurt in a land not your own?

The blue of the sea is overwhelming, sweeping and lifting the soul out of my body. From there, I see myself cut open, revealing a scar in the form of a scattered poppy flower. Looking more closely, I note that the light pink of new skin has grown over the scar, sealing the pain to a ledger of far-distant memories. This image helps me to feel different—able to breathe and regain control over my body again. When I stand up and turn around, I am not only putting one step in front of the other, but I am actually walking forward.

Weightless. Heavy. I feel my blood thickening, dragging, clocking life and all thoughts. I will never be the same. Never only be one thing no more. Tainted. Painted in colors which speak of unhappiness and loss; they connect the fickle soul to the oldest narrative of humanity. Stories of betrayal, redemption and fragile happiness, over and over in what appears to be an endless node made of human souls. Born from pain, we rivet for joy. And then one day—at first similar to any other—suffering crawls up and clenches the heart with sharp broken wings; a sudden reminder of the birth stretch, and the end of it all. How then to leave the human race and become a star made of dust, with no memory and the ability to burn without pain or need for purpose?

I remember these few lines Amory shared with me some time ago, and I only seem to understand them now, when I start feeling freed of their meaning. For the first time in a very long time, I did not desperately wish for stardom. At first, the change in me was imperceptible. The poet would ask to have another glass of wine, but I would feel tired and instead want to go to bed. He would hold my hand long after he pulled me off the street to avoid an accident with a crazy tricycle driver. I did not tell him about Xavi in too many words anymore, or how I felt I was starting to heal. Without Xavi paper-thin under my skin, it however lost its dullness. My movements appeared lighter and more refined because I no longer required superhuman efforts for my next step.

I think my newfound lightness moved the poet and inspired him to try shaking off his former ghosts, too. Patri, I wish I could better express how I truly feel the sea took pity on me. The poet sat next to me when I had my eyes fixed on the sea. If he did not sense the healing colors, I could not help him. And very subtly, I pushed back. Pushed back the attention I craved for before but never admitted to wanting. I was feeling sentimental during our last night in Coron as I felt a chapter in my life was about to end. It hit me that change is difficult by default. So, when the poet kissed me that night, I felt the universe turned silent for a moment, and I kissed him back. But when I looked at him again in the dark, his face merged with all the faces of the people I'd met in the last year, and I knew it was time to say goodbye. He took my hand and asked me to stay with him to celebrate our last night. When the night sky resumed conversing on gravity, light and distances too far to travel, I decided to simply go back to my own room. Does growth feel like this? Kisses, L.

Of Lightness and Clouds
10 September 2009

Dear restless nomad hearts, I've just returned from the Philippines. Interestingly enough, my father's home gave me closure on an unexpected topic. I thought I was over my break-up. The reality is that Bangkok was the perfect place to be distracted from it all. I was close by the sea when I felt this old wound truly closing, and when I also decided to leave my anger behind. Do you believe it is a coincidence that it happened in my father's birthplace? On the plane I wrote down a few words. They are very personal.

White nights

you made me change skin like no other. rip flesh off frozen mangoes. eat razors like candy. strip me bare inside out. starve me until I am cold air falling vertigo-nights deep. until I am fingernails tasting of blood and blades.

you hang my heart out to dry. feed it to the shark in my stomach. scream until my teeth are the color of pomegranate tea. wound me until I turn warrior queen; until we are splinted bones on the floor.

she asks for the size of my thighs. the color of my sprinting eyes. the name of my animal mouth with cracked skin on the inside. listening to the soft whispering of her voice, I turn around and lay down my knife.

And with finding peace, I want to express again how grateful I am for all your encouraging notes. Now, I am very excited to share a short story by the lovely marion_81. Let's not stop searching for love.

I slid and ended up in one of the small potholes on the roads, my feet and legs drenched by last night's rain. Luckily, I did not hurt myself and kept walking to work. I moved to Yaoundé in Cameroon only a month ago to work on a reforestation project.

That evening, my friends took me to Mont Fébé, one of the seven hills on which the town of Yaoundé is built. *Habibi, habibi* played on the car radio and for the first time. I focused not on avoiding potholes or making sense of the new world around me, but on standing completely still. From above the hill, the colors of the city are captivating. Bright red earth competes with lush green bushes, painting a spectacular picture with a mix of white simple buildings.

I marvel at how quickly acquaintances become friends in this place. Under the premise of feeling like an outsider, so easily spotted and unable to disappear into the crowd (la blanche/white girl—come here), friendships flourish. Tonight, Ramin joined our usual group. He had just relocated from Madrid for a short-term assignment with an international gas company. My routine check of his hands did not indicate any commitments. As the night continued, we moved on to Safari, the city's biggest nightclub. Couples danced in impassioned embrace and the DJ played songs on request. Ramin and I took to the dance floor with silly moves and laughter. Before saying goodbye, he gave me his number on a paper napkin, which I quickly folded and put in my bag.

The next day was a typical Yaoundé Sunday—one that begins with brunch with friends that melds into pool games and later dinner. I was still feeling the excitement of meeting someone I liked, and digested these feelings with my friends. Do I text him? Do I not? They each pitched in, one piece of advice more practical or ludicrous than the next. After debating the entire lunch, I finally just sent him a text asking if he wanted to have coffee with me the following week. Waiting for his text, which never came, made the day even slower.

He finally texted me back on Monday saying that he was out of town for work and had intermittent phone and internet access but that he would be back on the weekend and would see me at the National Day event at the French Embassy. My heart dropped when I saw him in a dark suit at the party. He was way more beautiful than I remembered. He smiled and walked across the room to greet me.

That night, as so many before, ended at Safari. We decided to drive out of the city the next morning. We drove out of Yaoundé in an open truck and onto long dusty roads. When we hit a bumpy trail, he took my hand to prevent me from falling. I kept holding on long after. Blue sky, the warm sun, his hand in mine—Lou Reed's "Perfect Day" in my head. The weeks flew by and I was still holding his hand. I knew then that I felt attached.

For him, all was very clear. We were what we were in Yaoundé, and that would end as soon as one of us left the city. For me, it was all a blur really. I knew our time was limited and I worried about how I would hold up once it was time for him to return to Spain. The night before he left, I could not hold back my thoughts. I told him I wanted to make it work, that I was willing to follow him to Madrid. From the way he looked at me, I knew that his fortitude and certainty cracked—if only for a moment. He did not answer, and I knew that was the end of the conversation. He had already made the decision to set us free. Free from the trappings of a long-distance relationship—emotionally bound but physically apart with both left to long in limbo.

I brought him to the airport. I could not speak, only hold his hand during the entire ride. I thought to die, when he embraced me what felt for the last time and disappeared behind the immigration line. The following day felt endless, interrupted only by an afternoon pool and game party, purposefully organized by my friends to distract me.

Food poisoning kept me in bed for three days. It was a mix of emotional and physical pain and a good excuse to avoid reality. A reality that included a well-paying but incredibly boring job. Ramin's presence had made me forget how underwhelming my professional life here actually was. With him gone, the world felt smaller, made up of fewer choices. Too late to completely reinvent my career, too late to become a doctor or an engineer. The same seemed true for relationships. Too few choices, too late to find the one. Maybe, I thought, I have already met all the people important in my life.

There were moments in the day when I felt completely fine and then, when least expected, the heartbreak would hit me. And it hurt. I occasionally heard from him, all happy stories about how he enjoyed his work, and Madrid, and its culture and food. Months went by. And then, out of the blue, I received an invitation from a former roommate from my exchange year in Spain many years ago. She was getting married in Madrid, and would I please be her guest? The answer was, of course, yes.

I took the metro from the airport and had to change trains in the Puerta de Sol station. The loudspeaker blared the announcement for the incoming train—*Tengan cuidado para no introducer el pie entre coche y anden* (be careful to not place your foot between the train and the station platform), when I saw him on the opposite platform. My heart jumped and body went numb, but still I managed to lift my hand and attempt a wave. He looked straight at me, but his face was blank. Only seconds before entering the train did he seem to recognize me. I was shaking—did this mean anything? I've always believed thoughts to be energy gliding through concrete structures and pulling the like-minded to randomly meet in urban spaces. Or maybe that's just wishful thinking. I finally arrived at my friend's house, where my thoughts were quickly interrupted by our warm reunion filled with loud chatter, catching up and wedding details. Still, when I woke up, he was in my head; and he had been there for a while. I decided to call. First there was silence, then I could hear a smile. He suggested we meet the next day for late afternoon drinks in *La Chueca*.

The colors of Madrid were darker than our sun-drenched days in Yaoundé, and he also seemed different from the picture of him I kept in my mind. He was distant and more serious, concerned with so many nuisances of a regular life back home. Or maybe our life in Yaoundé had been unreal —a time-bound break from our responsibilities in life, which made us ready to embrace people and time so easily. At the same time, I felt I wanted to join him where he was now, where life was real and where he grew to become mature but still so beautiful a man. I shared with him how all this time he stayed on my mind. These days when I could feel his sadness, his joy just by the way he started writing his notes to me—even the ones he did not write. He is quiet at first and then holds me and lightly kisses me on the neck. I dare. I jump. I say yes. To Madrid. To him. I know it is me carrying us. But I feel like I finally have a glimpse of the person hiding behind this wall of confidence and calm, right where the soul starts stretching. And it feels sufficient.

I returned to Yaoundé determined to get a job in Madrid. It took me five months to find a decent posting—not particularly a dream job but good enough. A serious last night of partying at Safari with mad dancing, laughter and some tears, and I was out.

It took me weeks after arriving in Madrid to adapt to the faster lifestyle, long hours at work, bustling crowds, and the overabundance of basic choices. But I fell deeply in love with him, our life and the city. And he was finally, truly, falling for me too. One year passed so quickly that I only remember lightness in the most meaningful way.

It was a Sunday night and, as usual, we spent it drinking wine and having tapas at La Latina, when I received a phone call from my mother. She was sick, and the doctors had given her very little time. Overwhelmed, I told him about it and he immediately encouraged me to move back to New York to be with her. The following weeks went by quickly. I quit my job and found consultancy work on 62nd street in New York, as well as a small apartment. Between the anxiety for my mother's health, stress of packing up my life in Madrid and starting a new one in a different city, I tried to ignore the sadness and emptiness I felt and wondered how my whole life could have changed in only a few days. When I finally left, he said, *"Grace, I'll carry us this time,"* and asked his company for a transfer to the New York office.

I saw a missed call from Ramin on my phone when I woke up. I immediately knew it meant bad news. He said his visa for the US got denied. There is no real explanation, other than maybe the sound of his name. Our lives seemed to submerge on parting skies. I was expecting tears. Instead they condensed and assembled into a cloud around my heart, keeping the sadness and anger from spiraling out of control. I smiled at work and wondered if I was able to draw everyone into my cloud or if someone realized that I had actually faded, transformed into a mere reflection of myself. Day after day, the cloud swallowed all joy. Until one day I saw a Facebook update by one of our friends we met in Cameroon saying she had been posted to the US Embassy in Madrid. I pick up the phone, beg and plead with her, and finally the tears come freely. It took weeks, but Ramin's visa was eventually granted.

I wait restlessly for him at the apartment until he finally arrives. When I open the door, he stands there holding a brown leather bag. He drops it on the floor and picks me up. It feels like lightness is finally closing the sky.

Lovely dreams, fellow nomad stars! Yours, lil_sea_girl.

3

GLO-CAL RELATIONS

I am searching for footsteps. A touch of this foreign land on me. My sweat on new old ground. A trace. Of. Fusion. You and me, country of residence. What have I learned? Did you listen? Are we alike? Separated through the space-time continuum of culture and development. United in matters of the heart. When the bubble bursts and true encounters begin.

From: Leya.Nunez@gmail.com
To: Patricia.Nunez@gmail.com
Date: 30 October 2009. 22:59 (Beijing time)
Re: first impressions

Patri, I have been hanging out in Beijing for a few weeks now. My internship with Taobao will start next week. In the meanwhile, I enjoy meeting so many eclectic people all over the city: businesswomen, diplomats and artists inspired to leave a mark. I was introduced to Fu Liu through a common friend at one of these events. I think he became my boyfriend somewhere along several surprisingly pleasant dinners. Our first dinner was funny. He promised to bring me to the finest hotpot place in Beijing. We ordered plenty of dishes, including tiger prawns, my favorite. I told him about that restaurant in Barcelona where they serve the best shrimps. The best in the world, I told him. While I finished my story about how you and I would make up stories to convince Maman to bring us more often to the restaurant, I realized that the skewered prawns I was about to put into the boiling hotpot in front of me were still moving their antennas. I screamed. "Are they still alive?" I asked. He frowned. "Of course. I told you this is a good restaurant. Do you think I would offer you dead seafood? We don't eat dead seafood here." He was obviously annoyed. The evening was not off to a good start. It's safe to assume he will not bring me back to a hotpot restaurant any time soon. After our dinner, I brought him to a bar in Xinsi Hutong, one of the oldest streets in Beijing, lined with traditional Chinese one-story houses. He had never heard of the bar before. We talked about our families and friends and avoided the topic of animal treatment in China. After we left, I grabbed his hand in the dark Hutong alley and kissed him. At first he seemed surprised but then leaned me against the cold stone of one of the neighboring houses and returned my kiss.

The Global Nomad Club
Speaking through walls
3 November 2009

Dear restless nomad hearts, I am excited to write my first blog from Beijing. I moved here by the end of September and am thrilled by the city, its contradictions and hidden beauty—buildings old and new, communism and market economy, protests and silence, hipster optimism and face masks almost everywhere. Walking through its old alleys and the Chinese architectural hutongs, I noticed a writing on the wall the other day saying *Fuck the city*. I imagined it'd been written by a foreigner having a really bad day in China. Maybe his electricity was cut off and he lacked the language skills to get the power back on. And after leaving his dark apartment was run over by someone on a bike? It made me think that global nomads and local residents often avoid or are unable to speak to each other. They do, however, have a point of view and leave each other messages on city walls. I want to thank sri_76, who sent me the picture of another graffiti, which had appeared overnight on a wall in Manila. It is a drawing of a Caucasian child and the bears the words *Foreign Invasion*. Was the artist blaming foreigners for rising living costs or did they despise the privileged and detached life many of them live? But the opposite holds true as well. Foodie_78 sent me a picture of all the writings of appreciation by foreigners on the wall of a small restaurant in Beijing. There are always two sides to every conversation! And my conclusion for now? Even if we disagree on politics and lifestyle, most of us concur on the importance of sharing good food.

Sleep tight, fellow nomad stars! Yours, lil_sea_girl.

From: Leya.Nunez@gmail.com
To: Patricia.Nunez@gmail.com
Date: 23 December 2009. 20:47 (Beijing time)
Re: the boyfriend

My dear, as promised, more on Fu Liu. The first surprising thing about him was that he accompanied me to the hairdresser. In Europe, I could never imagine a boy watching me cut my hair. I told him it would be boring. He insisted, so who was I to rebuff a slightly odd but rather sweet gesture?

We went to a salon in the central *Sanlitun* area. I caught him obsessively looking at himself in the mirror. When he was bored with his reflection, he would play with the zipper of the new black quilted bag he gave me a few days back. His hair is carefully combed to point straight up, his cheekbones are wide, and his face is pleasant. He dresses well. That day, he combined black skinny pants with a simple denim shirt. I did not see it going anywhere, but I felt comfortable with him. All his superficial attention made me feel taken care of. My heart is safe with him, out of his reach while my poppy-flower scar continues to fade. To survive Beijing's freezing winter of up to minus 17 degrees, it is essential to have someone caring. I know I am novel and exotic to him, excitement from a different world more than anything. But I like his carefree attention anyway. He's been showering me with clothes, bags and all the free time he has during his gap year.

He is trying to figure out his life. I think this is what attracted me to him. I understand how it feels to not know exactly what you want, to constantly have the perfect life goal elude you really. He promised his father that he would self-reflect after crashing his car at an illegal street race in Vancouver last year. There was the alcohol, days spent in bed, and endless video gaming, too. After college in Vancouver, he was called back home to China, leaving behind a girlfriend and close group of friends. I wondered if it was a specific event that triggered his downward spiral into recklessness or if emptiness had just slowly crept up on him. I imagined him living in Canada, faced with unprecedented personal freedom and far away from home, which must have challenged the meticulously planned life thought out by his demanding parents. He said he had veered off trajectory and for some reason could no longer return to the starting point he was in when he left Beijing several years ago. He felt torn between a world he knew so well but could not whole-heartedly return to and an unexplored alternative way of living life, in which I seemed to play a role. Sometimes I seem to catch glimpses of suffering on his face. It might be the duress of having to face his father week after week admitting defeat in turning his life into a success. The truth is that I'm not sure if he truly cares—maybe his visits to the old man are just a nuisance to him—but I quickly brush these feelings aside.

Several days ago, I asked him about the upcoming Chinese moon festival, which he celebrates with his family. Would he invite me to the family celebration so I could meet them? I wanted to eat mooncakes with different fillings and admire the round full moon with him. Would they mind that his girlfriend is a foreigner? He said his mom would like me. After a long pause, he said it was not appropriate to intro-duce me to his parents just yet. I asked him if he was ashamed of me. "Of course not," he replied. To make up for it, he invited me to a huge wedding of one of his former schoolmates from the international school in Beijing. I asked a friend to give me some fashion advice and he insisted I wear a traditional Chinese qipao dress. I selected a very subtle flower pattern on green silk and had the tailor on my street make it. I was extremely excited when Fu Liu sent over the driver. When we arrived at the wedding banquet, I realized not a single person was wearing tradi-tional Chinese attire. I definitely looked like the girl who was trying too hard. I smiled at everyone the whole night—it is, after all, the Chinese weapon against embarrassment—and clasped his arm very tightly. When we later headed outside to admire the fireworks, everyone complimented me on my dress. I can't figure out if they truly meant it. Much love, L.

The Global Nomad Club
Happy new year!
1st January 2010

Hey there, restless hearts, I wish everyone a very happy new year. I spent all day in bed, sleeping off last night and contemplating new blog posts. I did think back to when I created the blog. I was really at my lowest point in Bangkok (some of you may remember), and I wanted to reach out to others far away from home. In the beginning, I very much looked at what is similar in our experiences. Over time and discussions with many of you, I began to see the differences in our stories. The blog is meant to be a venue to tell a multitude of stories. Once more, I do wish you a very happy new year, and most of all answers to your questions in life. Please do send me your stories—the blog depends on it.

Good night, fellow nomad stars. Yours, lil_sea_girl.

From: Leya.Nunez@gmail.com
To: Patricia.Nunez@gmail.com
Date: 11 March 2010. 02:39 (Beijing time)
Re: Play

Patri, how are you feeling these days? My friend Marie, a visiting cultural director at the Alliance Francaise, recently invited Fu Liu and I to a photo exhibition called *Play* by a famous Chinese artist a few months ago. We took some friends of ours along with us. Anyway, the exhibit was composed by huge photographs of colorful things. I was not impressed. I went up to the artist to discuss his exhibition. I

wanted to know what he meant to say. He said it was a
critique on oversupply and consumption of cheap colorful
things in China. We got into a heated argument (about
what?). At one point, more and more people turned their
head around and joined our discussion. Suddenly, I realized
Fu Liu had disappeared from my side. I found him outside.
Our friends were gone. I asked him what happened in there
and he replied, "Nothing." When I prodded and asked him
where our friends were, he snapped and said they left. Why?
I was puzzled. Was it because of what I did? I asked him if I
embarrassed him because I criticized the artist's work, and
things went downhill from there. "Would you dare to speak
in the same manner to my parents?" he yelled at me. I yelled
back, "What have your parents to do with anything?" He
kept going. "I know in your culture you say what you think,
but in my culture, we respect the elder. He is a very interna-
tionally respected artist and it made me feel really uncom-
fortable. I couldn't believe it. I told him you are so
brainwashed." "The artist and I just had a really good
discussion. And why do you bring up culture now? I can't
believe you were embarrassed of me and accuse me of
insulting your parents. I wanted to meet them as a matter of
respect for them, and your culture, but you refuse to invite
me to meet them. I don't get you." I wanted to further
discuss it, but he completely shut down and ordered a taxi to
take me home. At this point I was so incensed that I refused
his transportation and met up with my friend Tate at a small
bar in the hutongs instead. Tate was in Beijing for the night
before heading out to Heilongjiang for work. I told him that
I thought culture was this convenient box everyone likes to
use when things do not go according to expectations.
Anyway, I was not sure what it was. He agreed with me and
we ordered more drinks. I imagined Fu Liu retreating back
into his world, ordering bottles at a major Beijing club,

feeling in charge while giving out champagne to a set of unremarkable acquaintances.

The Global Nomad Club
Apéro in Zurich
13 May 2010

Hey there, restless nomad hearts, how are you all tonight? I was contemplating the nature of relationships between local residents and global citizens when I received a very interesting piece from zurina_555, capturing the complex relationship between the Swiss and the Germans. Unknown to me, there seems to be an uneasiness about Germans in Switzerland. What prejudices and discrimination have you experienced during your journey?

Apéro in Zurich

The orange juice incident took place in Zurich. A Swiss friend—let's call him Matis—was then working as Vice President of Strategy with one of the big Swiss banks. He and a German colleague—let's call her Karin—were moving to another department in the bank and decided to organize a farewell apéro together. An apéro is the Swiss way to celebrate promotions, birthdays and farewells with colleagues. It usually involves wine, juice, sandwiches, croissants and sweets. Many bakeries around Zurich's financial center at the Paradeplatz specialize in catering for these events.

But Karin and Matis have different ideas of what their apéro should be. Matis wants to have it catered; Karin suggests making homemade sandwiches—it comes out much cheaper that way, she says. He frowns, quickly estimating her generous annual salary and bonus, but eventually concedes since she offers to do all the work. The following day, Karin bombards him with phone calls for approval on further cost-saving measures. Fed up, he hangs up on her and tells his colleagues about Karin, the stingy German. "Next thing you know she will ask me to stretch the orange juice with water." Whether or not the orange juice at this apéro was indeed watered down became a workplace urban legend.

Then there is the boss of Matis and Karin. Let's call him Frank. Frank, a tall blond German, has been leading a multi-cultural strategy team of five Swiss and four Germans for the past 2 years. After a few glasses of Neuchâtel Rose wine at Matis and Karin's apéro, he says, "I should probably not say this, but you Swiss suffer from an obsessive consultation culture. At times I do rounds of consultations even when the decision has already been made." An awkward pause follows. Colleagues on both sides of the cultural fence force a grin. Frank's telephone rings and he excuses himself from the apéro to attend to an important call. Everyone rushes back to their workstations, relieved he is gone. The next morning Frank makes amends and brings in gipfeli (known as croissants outside Switzerland) for breakfast. He says, "I have to admit that the work culture here is more inclusive and more collaborative. It will be hard to work for a German company again." Everyone nibbles on their gipfelis, nodding.

Karin and Frank are among the approximately 300,000 Germans who have immigrated to Switzerland. They consti-tute the second largest minority after the Italians. In Zurich, they represent the largest group of foreigners. Most German immigrants came to fill in job vacancies for which there were either no qualified nor interested Swiss candidates. The influx of Germans into Switzerland is attributed to a variety of reasons, including higher salaries and similarities in languages, and made possible by the Schengen treaty of free movement of labor. Germans and German-speaking Swiss share a written language but have distinct oral dialects. In a recent study by Dr. Thomas Koellen from the University of St. Gallen[1], a survey was conducted with 1,000 Germans working in Switzerland. The study notes that the influx of Germans has slowed in the last years. While this might be a reflection of the strong German economy, Koellen ponders if the unfavorable climate and bias against Germans living in Switzerland has contributed to the decline. His survey reveals intriguing findings: 30% of Germans living in Switzerland do not feel welcome or integrated. The degree of perceived rejection is subjective and varies substantially across respondents. Nevertheless, more than 50% of respondents agree in various degrees with the statement that one may not arrive as German but is made into one in Switzerland. Karin is suspected of cutting costs to the point of stretching her orange juice because she is German, not because she might simply be a little annoying. In Germany, she is simply Karin. In Switzerland, she is German Karin.

So, what exactly is the image of Germans in Switzerland? Koellen explains it spot on. The German, in his or her most caricatured version, is a bit too loud and demanding, with a Prussian military zack-zack (chop-chop, do-it-now) mentality. As a result, many Germans live alongside the Swiss rather than with them. Politically, the backlash against migrants—many of them highly skilled, such as the Germans—has shifted the Swiss political landscape to the right. In February 2014, the Swiss government was forced through a people's referendum to draft legislation limiting the number of foreigners coming into the country from the

European Union (EU), in contradiction with Switzerland's bilateral agreements with the EU.

The perceived "Germanness" of the Germans reinforces the Swiss identity. I am defined through what I am not. At the same time, Germans tend to simplify the Swiss into a digestible figure, useful in explaining the new surroundings. How are the Swiss perceived by the Germans living in Switzerland? As Frank candidly—and awkwardly—divulged at the apéro, the Swiss are seen as slow and stoic, like their surrounding mountains, pathologically inclusive or rather unable to take decisions at all. And what about their funny accent? Frank and Karin sometimes gather with other Germans over drinks at the Odeon, an upscale bar in Zurich, to complain about the Swiss and share their experienced micro-aggressions of the week.

As someone stuck between the Swiss mountains and the Prussian zack, my perspective embraces both sides. I grew up in Germany to a French Swiss mother and a German father and moved to Switzerland at the age of 21. Since then, I lived on and off in Switzerland and have never lived in Germany again. To be perfectly clear—the cultural differences between the Germans and Swiss are real. They were real at our family's dinner table and they are real at the shared workspaces at the Paradeplatz in Zurich. The key question is whether these differences become a hurdle in living together or they instead enrich the cultural subtext of a cosmopolitan city such as Zurich.

The perfidy of bias—gender, race, nationality, sexual orientation or religion—is that it is subtle, subjectively true as it is untrue. It is challenging to detect, isolate and prove, but it is hurtful, nonetheless. Often, there is a meta-level of hurt caused by well-meaning friends who want to convince you that it is really only in your head. It rattles confidence and fosters doubts on one's perception of reality. Is this person unfriendly because I am German or because she has a lousy day? In Koellen's survey, the respondents were equally divided in their perception of being discriminated—half felt they were, and the other half felt they weren't. Among my Swiss colleagues and friends, some have acknowledged the bias, and some say there is no problem. So, who is right?

Bias is most often real and not simply a by-product of the imagination. Yes, sometimes it really is just about a bad day —but it is also possible that an existing bias against Germans may feed into one's negativity on this particular day. Bias also equally exists on the receiving end and is referred to as confirmation bias, which is the tendency to interpret information in a way that confirms one's pre-existing beliefs. Once a person has been exposed to preju-dice or discrimination, she or he is more likely to expect and interpret another exchange as being unfairly biased. How does one best deal with overlapping realities around bias and the perception of it?

A good place to start is by accepting that we are all suscep-tible to it. People decide in 20 seconds if they like someone; it takes a Swiss 5 seconds to detect a German by his or her accent. There is a good chance that the negative image of "Germanness" will affect a Swiss person's first impression of new German acquaintances. On the flip side, many Germans expect the Swiss to have prejudices and hence expect interactions with them to go a certain way. Bias is rooted in an instinct to render the world less complex by identifying the same as friend and the other as enemy. While this instinct may have aided our survival in the early days of humankind, it is not particularly useful nor accurate in our societies today.

To bridge cultural divides, it helps to explain differences and put them in perspective. For example, one important explanation for the differences in tone and management style between Germany and Switzerland is the size of professional networks. In Switzerland, any given professional network is small, and professionals are bound to work together repeatedly. As a result, there is more incentive to collaborate. In Germany, the professional networks are much larger and the chances to work together again are slim. This promotes less cooperation. Thus, are they really that different in the end or merely reacting to different incentives? There are many more such explanations on differences in work culture.

In the end, it is simply a matter of choice. If we engage, we become of each other. We adapt the positive, challenge our regular way of going about life, and through this process grow into a more conscious and reflected version of ourselves. If we choose not to engage, we don't have to change, but we also don't learn. The urban fabric of Zurich and other Swiss cities is changing and stretching to include new migrants. If we embrace them, new ideas and alternative ways of living will transform cities into sounding more vibrant than ever. Cheers to that with orange juice—not stretched with water, that is.

Good night kisses, fellow nomads! Yours, lil_sea_girl.

My Eid al-Fitr in Mindanao
29 June 2010

Hey there, restless hearts. Beijing is sweltering hot and, just in this mood, one of the readers of this blog, Gabriela Blatter (gabrielablatter3), sent me this piece about her attempt to understand more about the local culture in the Philippines, her host country. Thank you for sharing!

My Eid al-Fitr in Mindanao

— GABRIELA BLATTER

Mindanao. Southern Philippines and home to the country's Muslim minority. Rich in biodiversity, natural beauty and untapped mineral wealth. A region with a long history of internal conflict rooted in religious differences, disputes in land and other natural resources and identity issues of the region's indigenous population.

Not knowing what to expect exactly, I boarded a plane and arrived midday in San Vicente. A friend from AFS Intercultural Programs, an international youth exchange organization, organized for me to stay with a guest family in Mindano for a weekend in order to experience Eid al-Fitr. The Eid festival ends the fasting month of Ramadan and is the most important Muslim religious celebration of the year. San Vicente is in majority Muslim and far enough from the conflict areas that it is considered safe.

Why did I sign up for the trip? As a Swiss scientist living in the Philippines for a short-term assignment, it was my first time to live in a country with a Muslim minority. I wanted to experience Eid closely within the Muslim community. I'm not very religious myself, but I wanted to understand the culture better by experiencing the most important Muslim religious festival. I had attended Hindu pujas when living in India and found that religion is often a good way to understand culture. All of this went through my head but was quickly brushed aside when I was picked up at the airport and driven to my guest family.

My hosts were a family of eight who had unsuccessfully tried for an entire year to accommodate an exchange student. I could not help but think that their Muslim faith and the number of children in the family might have played a role in the decision of the Christian faith-based AFS. My host family, in particular my host mother, was eager to show me all aspects of their culture. We started with pineapple picking, and a visit to the fish market. During the drive, I learned that my guest family belonged to a sect of Islam which celebrates Eid a day earlier than the majority of Muslims. They also celebrate only within their own nuclear family. Safety issues make it impossible for them to visit their relatives still living in the conflict-affected areas.

I told them that I did not bring appropriate clothes. Back home, my host mother and her girls took out many different abayas, a loose dress covering the entire body, with matching headscarves. I could not believe how excited they were to dress me up. Endless giggles and assurances on how much better I looked in these clothes. With my complexion, they said, I could pass for a beautiful Algerian woman.

We got up before sunrise on the morning of Eid. Everyone carefully bathed themselves with the available bucket shower. Just before leaving, my host mother noticed my painted fingernails and remarked on how I should be clean for praying and not wear nail polish. I thought about how I had made it a point to get my nails done before leaving for Mindanao in anticipation of the festival. Turns out it was the exact opposite of what I should have done. There was not enough time to remove the polish, but my host mother assured me it would not offend anyone.

The women and men of the family drove in separate cars to a soccer field in the middle of the town. It was heavily guarded by the army and was being searched for bombs. My anxieties were eased when I saw the easy, natural interaction between the people and soldiers. I observed the women. None of them wore nail polish. I did receive a lot of compliments for the abaya we finally selected, and my host mother seemed pleased.

Out of respect for the religion, I did not participate in the prayer and instead observed it from the sidelines along with other non-Muslim residents who were anticipating food hand-outs after the prayers. In the center stood the Imam, the religious leader, praying. The men of the community knelt before him. Separated by a wall around 2 meters high were the women, who sat in the back. When I later asked why men and women were segregated, I was told it was to maintain the concentration and solemnity of the ceremony and prevent them from being distracted by the opposite sex. Everyone prayed peacefully until sunrise. Once the prayer finished, we greeted and wished one another happy Eid. Then everyone, including the Christians, received food.

We returned home and the kids changed back into jeans and t-shirts. The host mother and I went from house to house. It is customary to break the fast with fruits (up to 25 different types) and salty dishes. As a foreigner, I was obliged to try 6 to 7 dishes at each home. I was surprised at how much they could eat after the prolonged period of fast. I was not the only non-Muslim, as Christian members of the community were also invited by the Muslim families. Additionally, many of the AFS families hosted foreigners and took them along to their Muslim neighbors. People reacted positively to my abaya and almost didn't even notice I was a foreigner since my hair was covered (otherwise, my blond curls would have given me away). A few Christians did not understand why, as a non-Muslim, I was even wearing an abaya. "Out of respect," I replied to them. Morning became afternoon and I took off the headscarf because of the heat. My host mother didn't mind. It seemed that everywhere I went, people were excited to meet a foreigner and ask questions.

I did not pay my host family for the stay and instead brought presents like Swiss chocolates and others. In return, my host family, who are in the jewelry business and relatively wealthy, gave me presents too—a bracelet made from wood beads and a set of jade jewelry. It was too much, but I thought it would be insulting to decline. I accepted with thanks. I asked my host mother why she was so interested in having an exchange student that she tried for an entire year. Her main motivation was to showcase her culture, she said. She felt that the perception of Islam in the West was not entirely correct. She wanted to help change this perception by demonstrating the peaceful practices and customs of Islam. Also, she added, it was a way of traveling for her without having to physically travel to Europe, which she could not afford. She asked me many questions about Switzerland and Western culture in general.

The next day I returned to Manila. I was glad to have escaped the city for a weekend to meet a truly great family and leave with a positive memory of my first Eid Al-Fitr.

Are you safely tucked in already, fellow nomad stars?! Yours, lil_sea-girl.

From: Leya.Nunez@gmail.com
To: Patricia.Nunez@gmail.com
Date: 22 August 2010. 22:59 (Beijing time)
Re: coming home

Patri my love, I'm at the airport now, alone and without Fu Liu. After our big fight, things cooled off for a while. It's funny. In every relationship, there is a moment when you see the first major flaw in the other. It sort of opens the floodgates to reevaluating their entire personality. I even started to get annoyed with the way he walked. It lacked a certain confidence and sense of purpose. I tried not to mind it so much because it seems so superficial—especially when writing it out like this, now. In any case, it's evident that our relationship is coming to an end now that I'm leaving for my last semester in Barcelona.

There were plenty of other moments after the fight, though, when he would reconquer my heart. One time, when I complained about my boss and how I wished she would give me more responsibilities, he picked up a daisy on the side of the street and put it in my hair. It could have been such a condescending and silencing gesture, but in the second we both quietly stood, it turned my perspective to see the beauty that exists rather than to continue obsessing about its absence in human relationships.

With the summer making way for fall, we found we had nothing left to discuss or decide. At one point in our relationship, I imagined I might be able to change my life for him and stay in China. But the truth is we did not have anything more in common than a shared understanding of family pressure to live a certain life. Together, I guess, we felt less alone, for a while at least. I did not propose to come back after Barcelona, and he did not ask me to return. But when he drove me to the airport, we were both sad. A piece of me stayed in Beijing, and I hope he and the persimmon trees we walked under hand in hand will remember my steps. Kisses, L.

4

WEIGHT

U s—*merging in global cities. Listening to ideas of its time. Weaken the source. Strengthen the individual. The nod. Fold existing structures. Reinvent space. Destruction. Fusion. Change. What do you do? Swimming. Waving. Standing still. Responsible for any of it?*

The Global Nomad Club
Returning home
22 September 2010

Hey there, restless nomad hearts, this is my first post after returning home to Barcelona. I will admit that returning home feels strange as I keep on missing the creative energy of Asia, the buzz, all the people. I also feel out of place here, humming and walking at a different rhythm than my old city. It's not to say that I don't love being home. I sleep a lot to unwire my brain from Asia and everything that happened while I was there. Slowly, I am falling back into my old routine of taking classes, studying and catching up with friends and family. When I first arrived, my stories felt stuck in my chest. It took time to come up with the words to describe the places where everything happened, such as my favorite food lane in Bangkok, the old alleys of Beijing or the silence of those Laotian temples. I also needed to create a multi-layered picture of my close friends, who are part of every story. And then it was partly the food, which brought me back! I had not realized how much I missed the food here. But the sentiment in the streets of Barcelona is depressing. Unemployment is at more than 40% among the young, and austerity dominates the news. Everyone is out in bars, complaining and trying to forget. I know I will leave again. It is far more than for the economic opportunities. I am not done exploring this big, complicated world out there. What about you? Are you thinking about your next step?

Sleep tight, fellow nomad stars! Yours, lil_sea_girl

From: Leya.Nunez@gmail.com
To: Patricia.Nunez@gmail.com
Date: 15 November 2010. 09:43 (Barcelona time)
Re: miss you

Darling Patri, you have left on vacations and now I am the one left behind for once. Last Sunday lunch with Mother and Abuela was both familiar and difficult. Familiar because there is always too much food and the endless chatter about family, friends and neighbors such as old Greta and her lost cat and how Mama thinks Greta is taking herself too seriously. Difficult because, at some point during the lunch, Abuela started yelling at me and calling me selfish for planning to leave Spain after graduation. It's been difficult to force a smile and explain that I am not like our father. I've told her many times that I love all of you and did not even know myself if this nomadic life was for me. Who knows if my next destination will be my last calling or if I am in fact our father's daughter, the seaman, always in search for new opportunities? But am I like him, irresponsible and not made for family life as Abuela implied? Come back soon. Hugs, L.

The Global Nomad Club
Graduation
3 July 2011

Hey there, restless hearts. I know it has been a while. Thank you for all your messages, comments and for sending me your own written work. I finally graduated last week but it has not given me the answers I was looking for. It has only raised more questions. Which field to build a career in? I wish being successful and powerful was a career choice instead of a goal. Which country or city to live in? How to get a job and the required visa? Whom to be with? I feel I have stalled. When I was at the beach last week with old friends, I sought out their direction. Most did not have an elaborate life plan and did not care about having one. My friends talked about leaving but without any serious intentions. Maybe to Germany? Does one need to speak German? They tell me I am lucky to have the international education and experience to be able to leave again. I know what they mean, but I can't help but feel uprooted and lost for now. Grateful for any pointers, shared experiences and comments.

On a completely different note, I had forgotten about the light here. I reconquer my city by running until I find myself fully immersed in the warmth of the early morning sun. *There, I finally feel your pulse again, Barcelona!*

Buenas noches, fellow nomad stars! Yours, lil_sea_girl.

The Global Nomad Club
To Live where Life is Precarious
7 September 2011

Hey there, restless nomad hearts. I am writing about a very personal topic today. I've been chatting with someone from the Global Nomad Club community, Stefan Bigler (stefan-bigler_787), about how the global life imprints on the soul. This piece is for all my fellow nomads in challenging places. But I believe even those of us in global cities—that are considered relatively safe—know the footprint on our bodies and minds, the physical scars from moving and getting injured in unknown surroundings (including the heart), as well as the moments of magical excitement inherent to every new beginning[1].

To Live where Life is Precarious

— STEFAN BIGLER

My sense of adventure and the urge to do something meaningful, something that makes a difference, inspired me to become a humanitarian worker. I participated in four humanitarian missions with the International Committee of the Red Cross (ICRC) from 2009 to 2014. First, I was posted in the Northern Caucasus—in the restive Russian republics of Chechnya and Dagestan. Then, I worked in the very traditional Pashtou lands in the North of Pakistan, close to the border with Afghanistan. My third mission brought me to the Central African Republic, a country most of us struggle to locate on a map, despite of years of violence and armed conflict. Finally, in 2014, I was posted in Donetsk, Ukraine, for a couple of months.

The same ideals kept me motivated but were in many ways put into perspective throughout the different missions. Adventure was an important motivation for me. I admit that the element of adrenaline is addictive, the feeling of being at the pulse of life and part of something that is bigger than yourself. With time, I have become more realistic and less prone to romanticizing humanitarian work. One gets used to the lifestyle and it becomes a job. Not an ordinary one but, in the end, still a job. It is important to me to have meaningful work, although I now also understand its limitations. I have realized how little an impact we have in the greater scope of things, but at the same time how important this small impact can be. To do good remains an important gratification; I call it the wanting-to-do-good syndrome. In the end, however, it all comes down to personal motivations and preferences. The deeper motive remains egoistic as in all our actions. Various people I met have lost their idealism over time. Some just enjoy the good life and perks of living and working in developing countries such as living in a big house and having household help. Others become cynical. Some openly admit that money is their main motivation, others have nowhere else to run. Yet, I met plenty of highly motivated staff to look up to in the humanitarian world.

The experience that marked me most as a humanitarian worker is also the hardest to describe and articulate. The Central African Republic (CAR) is without doubt the most difficult and emotionally charged mission for me. In March 2013, a coalition of rebels—the Séléka—brought down the government. The country quickly descended from an already fragile political and socio-economic situation into almost total chaos. Soon, counter-rebels formed, fighting the former rebels now in control of the country. At the same time the conflict transformed, and battles started to be fought along religious lines. The Séléka were in majority Muslim, and the counter-armed militias Christian. This I remember was the moment when the war lost all rationality for me. In Bouca, Christian militias attacked in the morning dawn. During the fighting with the Séléka rebels, a lot of people were killed, mostly civilians, including children and elderly people who couldn't flee. Hundreds of houses were burnt to the ground. When my team and I arrived two days after the fighting, some houses were still burning. Some rebels of the Séléka, who had repelled the attack and kept control of Bouca, rested in the shade under some mango trees. They seemed relaxed and yet puzzled at themselves. Like they had run out of ideas on how to make sense of what they did. I remained with only one thought—how this destroyed village with decomposing bodies in the open daylight represented the absolute lowest point of humanity. Several hundred Christians had taken refuge in the church of the village. The expectation these survivors placed in me and my team was overwhelming. They thought that because we were with them, they would be safe. And while I was hoping that this was the case, I had no assurance and it felt like a heavy responsibility. The fear and hate of the other was constantly present on both sides, and it was at times difficult to bear. Fortunately, I was too busy organizing assistance, so there was simply no time to indulge these feelings. I spent my days negotiating the protection of the living remaining in the church, burying the dead, organizing food distributions and overseeing medical evacuations. Emotions remained intense throughout our three weeks in the village. Some people had lost everything and yet they expressed their gratitude to us for saving their lives. On a personal level, this was incredibly moving.

I remember being surprisingly calm throughout the entire time. The constant stress trumped my fear. I was scared before we got there, but once we had reached the destroyed town, I relied on my earlier acquired skills to assess if a soldier could be trusted and to distinguish between an empty promise and a real assurance of security. While I was in Bouca, I did not dream once. Later, I frequently dreamt about the village and my time there. Processing the events took a lot of time. I dealt with it foremost by speaking to people from the ICRC. Every time I meet with them, the events of that time come up. I find it difficult to share this with people for whom such experiences are completely alien. I also truly believe there is a part that will always remain unprocessed, and to a certain extent it is part of a conscious choice to avoid rationalizing violence and suffering.

It was interesting how my perception of the world differed at times from the local population's. Repeatedly having been exposed to violence over many months, they expected armed men to be violent. Meanwhile, I kept holding on to the luxury of my worldview, in which people do not kill each other. It felt like we lived through the same events but saw them through different lenses. I do hope the country will eventually come to a state of lasting peace and stability. To again become a place where children dream of things other than mourning the dead and burning houses.

I connected most with the local residents of the Northern Caucasus, probably because of the greater cultural affinity. That people looked, talked and dressed similarly to me made our interaction easier. I still keep in touch with friends there. Yet there were also limits to the understanding. In particular in Chechnya, the role of women is very traditional. When I opened up about my liberal opinion on the role of the woman in society, a lot of my female officemates agreed. Some male colleagues as well. But there were topics incomprehensible to them such as women remarrying after a divorce. "But then, she is not a virgin anymore!" I did not try to change their opinion.

In Timergara, where I lived in Pakistan, women wear burkas when leaving the house. At the office there were no women, which was strange to me. There was clearly more mistrust toward me, a foreigner from a Western country, than in any other place I had lived in before. I remember that it was very difficult to talk about religion. I had to conceal being an agnostic even if they expressed their own doubts on religion and its practice. Usually, I was assumed to be Christian, and I left people in that belief. One evening, a colleague and good friend said, "I would like you to become a Muslim. It breaks my heart to know that you will suffer in hell when you die". In many ways, the town I lived in in Pakistan was very traditional, and not reflective of the country and its society at large.

In the Central African Republic, true interaction was made difficult by completely different economic realities. The majority of people are self-sufficient farmers and live in simple brick houses without connection to the global world through radio or television. Thirteen percent of children die before the age of five. Life's concerns are just so different. I felt they thought of me as the white person—a sort of an alien from a different planet. At times, I was the only white person in the village. There was truly no way to blend in. At the local market, I sometimes felt like an actor on stage and people were waiting for my performance. They never came close to me but I felt they quietly observed the stage on which a white actor bought his vegetables. Most did not distinguish between me and my other European colleagues. Over time, people lost interest.

I thought about returning home. I missed my family. My sister had had a baby and I realized I missed so many days of her life. I realized how life continues without us and how much of it I missed. I often felt alone and bored, and my living circumstances felt at times unreal and frustrating. I also saw my older colleagues who had been doing this for a long time and living in a really unhealthy and unsustainable way. But when I finally returned home, I was surprised how long it took me to reintegrate. I had trouble being interested in living again in Switzerland. Everything seemed too organized and the place missed a certain creative energy. What I saw during my humanitarian missions changed me. I developed a certain distance to my life in Switzerland. I still feel only 90% reintegrated and sometimes feel I do not fully belong. My perspective has greatly changed. Life is Switzerland feels indirect and withdrawn. It is not about survival but comfort and maximizing happiness. None of my friends have true problems, in the sense of what people deal with in the Central African Republic. Our discussions evolve around vacations, consumption and art. People complain a lot and I find myself intolerant toward this behavior. Once I saw two black soldiers on the train. They looked so small in their uniforms—just like the child soldiers I had seen so many times before. While I was immediately aware that they were Swiss soldiers performing their mandatory military service, I was still transported back to the village in Central African Republic, the beauty of the landscape but also its violence. Sometimes now, when I cook Thai, I think back on my garden in Kaga-Bandoro where I grew Thai herbs and vegetables from seeds that I got from a Vietnamese friend. Then I also wonder if the rucola I planted in my herb garden still survives. And I know there remains a longing to go back and work where life feels more meaningful.

❧

Stay safe! Yours, lil_sea_girl.

The Global Nomad Club
Floating
11 November 2011

Hey there, restless nomad hearts! Since graduation, all I've been doing is running and hanging out at the beach with my non-linear friends. But the silent stares from my family when I get home after another aimless day are starting to get to me. And I will admit to you that I feel lonely. They are too many options, which ironically makes it so challenging to seize one of them. I know that I am lucky to have these many opportunities, and still, I feel unsettled and anxious about my next step. A few days ago, I got a phone call from my friend A., who recently moved to San Francisco. We spoke for hours. He told me about job opportunities and the cultural vibe of the city. He said I could stay with him. Though I'm really in no financial position to fly to the US and sustain myself there for a long time, I've still decided to take the chance. I am desperate to see if the city could be a way out of this funk I've been in since returning home. Please do message about the city. I am thrilled about this new adventure. Stay tuned for new posts from San Francisco!

Buenas noches, my fellow nomad stars! Yours faithfully, lil_sea_girl.

From: Leya.Nunez@gmail.com
To: Patricia.Nunez@gmail.com
Date: 10 February 2012. 08:05 (San Francisco time)
Re: job

Hi! First the big news—I got a job offer from Jet.com, an e-commerce start-up. Second, I am officially in love with San Francisco. I am fascinated with people, the endless creative energy and its beautiful surroundings. The months before they hired me were admittedly tough. Most potential companies liked my background, but the visa situation is difficult, and they need to really like your profile to sponsor your H-1B visa. A few weeks ago, I went to a FWD.us event where Mark Zuckerberg spoke about the necessity to expand the caps on H-1B visa for highly skilled workers.

After the speech, I attacked the free food and looked around to see if I knew anyone. I must have looked slightly distressed because this guy walked up to me and told me he was only there for the free food too. Turns out I actually know him. His name is Nawin. Kat, a common friend (I met her while diving in Coron. He knows her from international school in Bangladesh.) put us in touch through email but we never actually got around to meeting up. We got into a heated discussion on immigration and the trends of rising xenophobia everywhere. I disagreed with his take on European immigration policies as having failed and countered that Americans tend to view Europe as a bloc while different countries have implemented different policies and experienced respective successes and failures. We agree that globalization and increased attempts at mobility have provoked a backlash, aiming to delay a process of greater mobility, which seems irreversible in the long run. I could not help but think back to Fu Liu and how he hated disagreements in public. Nawin and I had an instant connection and promised each other to stay in touch. I hope I will have more to write about him in my next letter. Love, L.

The Global Nomad Club
Good-bye and Arrivederci! Yours faithfully, the Young
29 March 2012

Hey there, restless nomad hearts. This is my first post since arriving in San Francisco. I have found a job and I love the city, but I can't forget my past few months in Barcelona. I think about my friends and family in Spain today, and how the economic crisis has affected so many lives and families in one way or another. None of my friends there could avoid the thought of leaving for a better place. Some stay either because they cannot or do not want to leave, others, like Ruben Barreto (rubenbarreto80), who is from Portugal and my co-author for this piece, have decided to leave.

> *Good-bye and Arrivederci! Yours faithfully, the Young*

— RUBEN BARRETO

Many young Europeans are leaving their native countries. The number of French citizens living abroad (1.6 million) increased by 60% since 2000. In 2005, there were about 300,000 highly skilled Italian workers living abroad in OECD countries, and these figures have likely increased in recent years.[2] As of 2013, approximately 285,000 Germans (equivalent to 0.7% of the workforce in Germany) live and work in Switzerland.[3] About 50,000 Germans live in Silicon Valley.

With an unemployment rate of around 10% of the working population and a youth unemployment rate of about 21%, European migrants are increasingly choosing destinations outside the EU. Switzerland attracts many of these migrants (net migration rate of 8.6 per 1,000 inhabitants during 2010–2013), as well as Australia, Canada, the Gulf states, and the United States.[4] As Europeans living in Asia for many years, we observed the increasing number of young Europeans looking for a better life in this booming region, in particular after the debt crisis.

Available data does not provide detailed information about skills level, but in most countries this generation of young migrants is perceived to be the best qualified ever, representing a significant public investment in education that is not bringing the intended benefit to the society that paid for it. For example, in Spain it costs the government an average of €60,000 to train an engineer, but many young Spaniards move increasingly frequently to neighboring countries within the EU, but also to developing countries, where local contracts are more attractive than wages back home.

To take a mere economic view—based on wage differentials —provides only a very limited explanation of this emigration pattern. In reality, humans move beyond national borders for a variety of reasons. In the version of young Europeans, it appears to be to find perspective of a brighter future, the creative energy of emerging economies, or the preference for a particular set of public policies. There are the stories of young French entrepreneurs moving to London because of the start-up-enabling environment and business orientation of the city. Young Italians moving abroad because Italy's job market is biased towards older workers, who enjoy job security, high salaries and the lion's share of responsibility. Young Germans disillusioned with the way the country is changing emigrate to places with less dysfunctional politics and public policies more aligned with their own views. Their personal decisions to emigrate is more than a number in the Eurostat statistic; it often carries the value of a political statement: they vote with their feet.

Does the emigration of mostly young citizens pose a challenge to democracies in Europe? Is voting with your feet expressing a voice by choosing exit as part of a healthy democratic process? Or does it in fact dilute traditional accountability mechanisms in contemporary democracies?

Currently these questions are mostly theoretical in that the numbers are still relatively small. But the number of young emigrés are rising fast and these countries are often losing some of their brightest. And while several countries allow their citizens to vote from abroad, others are not, and their voices need to be captured through alternative channels. To address skills shortages of their companies, the state of Bavaria, for example, organized specific forums to re-connect with their émigrés. This provided the space for an exchange of views. One could imagine more and other channels of providing a voice and a chance to listen to these émigrés. We need to think about adapting our democratic processes to the reality of a world with fewer obstacles on crossing borders and more restless citizens.

Sleep tight, fellow nomad hearts, lil_sea_girl

From: Leya.Nunez@gmail.com
To: Patricia.Nunez@gmail.com
Date: 3 April 2012. 21:13 (San Francisco time)
Re: Nawin

Patri love, sorry for my belated reply but I've been so busy at work. I know you want to hear more about Nawin. How do I begin? I first noticed his big dark eyes that seemed to look only at me. He asked me all these questions. Was I lil_sea_girl because of my father? Did I want to stay in San Francisco forever? How tall did I feel? What was the happiest day of my life? Or did I think it was yet to happen? Which magical skill would I ask for if I could? Which evil would I cure if I had superpowers? He did not stop asking, and I felt at ease answering each of his questions. It feels like he wants to know me in a way few people have made the effort to.

He was born to a Ghanian mother and a Bangladeshi father. Instead of choosing a name from either of their cultural backgrounds, they made up a name for their first son, creating their own new world for him to grow up in. In the language they invented only for him, Nawin means "the distinguished one." Maybe this is what allowed him to be such a special person, well... in my eyes anyway. He works as a bioengineer at VyoCycle, a medical diagnostics start-up. He is incredibly impressive, or so I tell him all the time. I don't even remember when exactly we started dating. Dating in the US is much more regulated and way too codified for my taste. I obviously ignored all of it and instead just hung out with him. It worked beautifully. One night, we met for drinks at a bar downtown, and when the bar closed, I invited him to my place. We talked and fell asleep in our clothes. Since then, he has not stopped asking questions. And I have asked him so many questions, too. If he preferred the mountains to the sea? Who did he think is the most inspiring leader of all time? Who or what has scared him? Did he think trees could have feelings, too? I told him about Bangkok and my time with the boys, and he was completely unfazed. He assumes I had my fun and am ready for the next big milestone in life. He told me about a few girls he was with, but honestly, I don't want to hear too many details. One of them mildly broke his heart.

Nawin and I just happened naturally and without force. It is a sharp contrast to how I used to always associate love with the exciting passion I felt for near strangers within a few weeks of delving into their souls and minds. Our story is simple. There are no other people. Our lives are so similar in design. He has many exciting plans for the future. His own company maybe. Children definitely. To possibly live in Ghana one day—would I be up for it?

He feels grounded, having embraced his mobile roots but also making a home everywhere he settles, albeit temporarily. I envy him for his family. They are warm, loving and always communicating. Sometimes I imagine building a similar kind of family with him one day. Of course, I am getting well ahead of myself. My brain is freshly in love, and by no means in the right place to make any life-altering decisions. I search for his flaws because our story just seems to be too good. I know I have to stop overanalyz-ing. But I could not help but notice that there was a shade of vulnerability missing from the color spectrum of his heart. Writing this out makes it sound even more stupid than in my head. I just cannot mess this up. Promise to talk me out of it. How are you, my dear? I really want to meet this new boyfriend of yours. Do you want to bring him with you to San Francisco? L.

From: Leya.Nunez@gmail.com
To: Patricia.Nunez@gmail.com
Date: 5 June 2012. 21:13 (San Francisco time)
Re:

Dear Patri, I am forwarding you an email I received a few days ago:

Lil_sea_girl, I've been following your blog for a while now and really feel I need to write to you. I think your blog does not represent a wide range of narratives, contrarily to what you claim in earlier posts. Albeit called the global nomad club, your blog feels self-centered and does not sufficiently highlight the plight of people experiencing huge challenges in moving, like me—people of color, of a different name or an undesirable passport. I have not left the US for years, as I am scared to not be re-admitted, and this although I have a valid student visa. It pains me very much to not be able to visit my family back home. I wish you could enrich the blog with more perspectives. Best, M.

I'll admit only to you that these words stung—and it took a while for me to admit that he is right. His comment made me feel silly—and somehow blindsided. I will address this on my blog very soon, but I don't know how. I do feel quite resigned, and a little embarrassed. But also, I know what you will say. Just ignore the blog for a few days, recover and get back to work. Of course, you are right. Take care, darling sister, L.

The Global Nomad Club
Not my story
27 Juni 2012

Hey there, restless nomad hearts. I want to share critique I received from one of you. This person feels the blog only presents a very privileged perspective, and shared the difficulties, injustice and humiliation experienced when attempting to cross borders. It made me stop and think for a while. I don't think I have the perfect answer, but I do want to reply. I have to agree to the extent that the blog is reflective of my experience, friends and readers. But at the same time, I would like to reiterate that my blog intends to be inclusive for all global nomad experiences. I would like to hear from you on how to make this happen. Everyone's story has a place on the blog!

Trying to do better and love you all. Yours, lil_sea_girl.

From: Leya.Nunez@gmail.com
To: Patricia.Nunez@gmail.com
Date: 8 September 2012. 19:27 (Borneo time)
Re: Borneo

Much love from Borneo! A week ago, we arrived at the orangutan sanctuary. This is the best pre-birthday gift ever. When I woke up this morning, Nawin was already gone. I found him swimming in the river. He only recently told me about a major personal crisis he had after two semesters at university. Questioning his entire life, including his studies, family and purpose in life, he moved to Borneo to live and volunteer at this orangutan sanctuary. Most staff and even some of the animals still seem to remember him. I can't even begin to picture him having any sort of crisis since he is always in control of himself and every situation and commands a room at ease. I am so glad I got to see and know more about him from the time we met. There are still old pictures of him on the wall of the main house. Back then, he did not wear his signature black frames. We sometimes squabble since I probably like the idea of getting dirty volunteering at camp more than I like getting actually dirty. But once we start observing these beautiful creatures, we forget everything. It is now and here that I finally see a vulnerable shade of orange on his heart, and as a result I fully connect and surrender any guard I might have still kept up in this relationship. Kisses, L.

From: Leya.Nunez@gmail.com
To: Patricia.Nunez@gmail.com
Date: 15 March 2013. 22:59 adapt (Napa time)
Re: wedding

Patri, I am sending you a few pictures of Amory's wedding here in the new world wine valley. It was a wonderful few days. Finally, Amory's inquisitive mind found a match in Aturo. An architect from Mexico living in San Francisco, he is an avid reader, just like Amory. The Nappa country constituted the perfect backdrop for a relaxed celebration. People from different phases of his life attended—even Saaki made it. She now splits her time between L.A. and Hawaii. There were a few moments when I pictured Nawin and I being in their place. And then again, I feel just happy to be in love, and not ready to think about the future in this way. Sending kisses, L.

The Global Nomad Club
Global City Magnet
17 April 2013

Hey there, restless nomad hearts. How is everyone? I was very busy with work lately, but I am glad to finally find the time to share with you a piece written by the beautiful Maciej Bugala (mbugala). Some of us move to global cities for work, others for love or urban culture. Maciej speaks about those moving for more fundamental reasons: civil rights in global cities. An important piece.

Global City Magnet (reprint)

— MACIEJ BUGALA

Sexual orientation, and the relative freedom to live openly and the possibility of equal marriage rights in liberal global cities such as London or New York, have an undeniable pull. At the same time, in many places persecution or non-acceptance of sexual orientation remains a serious issue. And not everyone is able or wants to move to liberal global cities. His piece takes a careful look on three persons who did come to London for these reasons. We might meet in global cities, but our narratives are different.

Mirek is 30 years old. Five years ago he chose to radically change what he called home by moving from his native Poland to London. "When I reached my early twenties, I realized there are certain aspects of my identity that can hardly meet with people's acceptance in Poland," he says. "And that if I wanted to feel free to actively express who I really am, I should move. Once I reached that conclusion, I had no doubts as to where I should live. London was an obvious choice."

What he refers to by "certain aspects of my identity" is his sexuality. Mirek is gay.

In conversation, he reveals stories from his past—oppressed urges and enforced compliance to a hetero-normative Catholic society and country. "It's not that I was unhappy then," he says of his life in Poland. "I simply didn't know I had the right to be happier. I thought of what I now perceive as my sexuality as something natural, but wrong, like kleptomania, for example. Some people naturally and inherently feel like stealing, but everyone agrees that stealing is wrong. It was only when I turned 20 that I realized that defining what I was as 'wrong' was doing me harm. And me sleeping with men who wanted the same thing was no harm to anyone." Then he adds, "It was quite the opposite of harm, to be honest. And I'm far too modest to call myself an altruist." He giggles.

Mirek makes a very interesting interlocutor. I struggle a bit with my Polish, not accustomed to using it for discussing abstract ideas and emotions. I think to myself, *not many people who speak this way stay in Poland.* Perhaps this thought makes me biased in the way I lead our conversation.

He makes self-depreciating comments, which at first may seem as stemming from insecurity, but as he continues talking, I realize it's his Polish cynicism. He nods his head when I suggest that growing up gay in a society prone to bullying taught him to make jokes first before anyone else could hurt him.

We are both educated to a level above the European average. Neither of us can claim to be a genius, but we are both definitely more clever than the proverbial John Smith (or, indeed, Jan Kowalski) and we both earn salaries above the median EU household income. Neither of us has ever considered moving back to Poland. Not because of our successful lives in London, but because of what we think would be a downgrade in our liberties. For him, because being gay in Warsaw is nowhere near as easy as being gay in London.

"Had I struggled to live in London, I would have considered going back to Poland despite the much lower levels of acceptance of gay people," Mirek explains. "But I'm comfortable here, and there is absolutely no reason to even consider such an option. I work as an academic. I earn enough to live comfortably, and I am surrounded by open-minded people who challenge me intellectually on a daily basis. I am happy."

Of course, brain drain is not a new phenomenon. Over the centuries, global cities have attracted millions of the intelligentsia from other parts of the globe. Continuing with Poland as an example, I think of the likes of Chopin (Paris), Joseph Conrad (London), Marie Curie (Paris), and Roman Polanski (Los Angeles). But right at the time when countries like Poland have the potential to keep their talent at home as the economies grow and living standards rapidly increase, the global cities remain one step ahead. And it's an important step, perhaps the most important of all: they allow you to be who you are. The brain drain of one is the brain gain of another.

Poland is clearly only a case in point. Amit is a gay Tanzanian, and despite Tanzania and Poland being so far removed from each other, our conversation leads me to conclude that both countries experience a migration of gay talent.

Amit is in his late 30s and has been living in London for over 20 years. His younger brother moved back to their home country years ago and married a local girl with whom he lives in his 10-bedroom house with a swimming pool on Tanzania's jewel island, Zanzibar.

Amit comes from a very privileged family of Tanzanians. His childhood was very different from mine, having spent his early years in a fully serviced household with two cooks, two gardeners, and multiple cars with chauffeurs. He went to a boarding school in England and eventually completed his undergrad at Cambridge. At the age of 23, his life was drastically "reduced" to my life: a gay Londoner with a foreign passport.

With all the honesty of my bias, this comes to me as a surprise. Abandoning a middle-class life in Poland is one thing but ditching the luxury of being part of a privileged class in one of the most beautiful corners of the world is something quite different.

Amit continues telling me about his current life. "I work as a musician for the English National Opera and I freelance doing jazz gigs. You know, jazz pays peanuts, but the ENO provides a good living."

He then tells me about his two female flatmates, with whom he shares a flat in the trendy neighborhood of Angel. He hasn't received financial support from his parents ever since he told them that he was gay and that he wasn't planning to go back to Tanzania. This was 15 years ago, and he hasn't been back since. He speaks to his mother regularly on the phone, but his father told him he would have him arrested if he ever showed up in Zanzibar. This might seem like drama created by a disappointed parent, but being gay is illegal in Tanzania and—at least in theory—punishment for same-sex "crimes" could be lawfully enforced.

Amit's story is very different from mine or Mirek's, but I suddenly realize that at the bottom of it lies the same cruel process that leads people away from their home countries: the desire for liberties and freedom of expression.

"Living in London is not always roses," Amit adds. "I've been verbally abused many times, once even while walking down Oxford Street—can you believe it? But the big difference is, I can do something about it here. Here, the law is on my side, not on the side of the abuser. And with that I can cope."

At the end of our conversation Amit mentions Freddie Mercury, and at first I find no relevance. He then tells me—to my great surprise—that the legendary lead singer of Queen was also from Zanzibar. I've known he was gay since I first saw him on MTV in the 90s. I wonder how many talented gay men and from how many countries around the world end up in London and stay here for the rest of their lives.

My third interviewee is neither an academic nor an artist. But he represents a rare breed of people, which countries like Poland, Tanzania, and the majority of the world has a deficit of: the charismatic ones.

Alessio comes from Naples, Italy. He is a human-rights activist affiliated with Amnesty International, who does a lot of campaign work around gay rights in West Africa. Sadly, as he says, "gay rights" in that part of the world usually means advocating for people jailed in Nigeria for having homosexual interactions.

Alessio's father is Nigerian. He and his parents moved back to Nigeria after Alessio completed his basic schooling in Italy. Naples was not a place to live for a black man. "If you're black, you can never be Italian, and my father is a very proud man with a strong need for belonging and community," he explains. "I went to an American high school in Abuja and then—at the age of 15—I managed to convince my parents to send me to a boarding school in the UK."

A lot of questions come up in my head: Why did you not want to stay with your parents? Why the UK and not Italy?

But I sense I am not the first person with these questions, since Alessio preempts them with an explanation. "I knew I liked other boys when I was 13. But I also knew I could never tell anyone in Nigeria about it. Italy was not a good option either, because having spent my childhood there I remembered how closed-minded and Catholic its people were; I would have been a double-outsider there—gay and black. I wanted to go somewhere free and somewhere where I spoke the language. The UK was the best choice." His last statement rings a bell and I suddenly remember Mirek saying, "London was an obvious choice."

Alessio is now in his late 20s and is determined to stay and apply for a British passport, even though as an EU national he is under no legal pressure to do so. "I want to belong to the country that allows me to be who I am," he explains. With this language, he makes me think of his daily duties as an Amnesty International campaigner. He sets up and manages public marches and protests against human-rights breaches around the world. I can easily imagine him standing in front of the Russian embassy in London with a sign "NO to anti-gay Olympics." I can't help but think that both Italy and Nigeria (and Poland and Tanzania...) will not change without people like him who have the courage and charisma to resist against the mainstream. This is perhaps the most hopeless and tragic side of the gay brain drain, which benefits cities like London and New York, but disadvantages the countries of origin of those who emigrate in search of civil rights.

Of course, simply identifying the lack of sexual liberties and freedom as an obstacle and a reason for the exodus of talent does not make it easier to address. Respect of civil rights is in a way beyond legislations and policies, and they remain out of the governments' influence. Poland's legal system indeed does not criminalize sexual relations between people of the same sex, nor does it allow discrimination of gay people. But the majority of Polish society does not necessarily define their perceptions based upon what is legally recognized as acceptable. Two men sharing a hotel room in Warsaw are many times more likely to encounter unpleasant comments from the receptionist than if they had decided to stay at a hotel in London. And as long as this continues to be the norm, the global hub-cities will continue to benefit from a brain gain at the cost of the rest of the world.

Don't sleep alone tonight, fellow nomad stars. Yours, lil_sea_girl.

From: Leya.Nunez@gmail.com
To: Patricia.Nunez@gmail.com
Date: 24 November 2013. 12:37 (San Francisco time)
Re: home

Dear Patri, I need to share some good news with you. Nawin and I moved in together. Before that, we had a huge fight about renting an apartment versus buying a house. I thought about our house in Barcelona, and how its inflexible foundation forcefully held our family together as we ate dinner together every night at the same time. Anyway, thinking about buying a home freaked me out but I could not admit that to him. Instead I made up arguments. What if we decide to leave San Francisco in 5 years? What do we do with the house then? Is it even a good time to buy? The newspapers have been reporting how Chinese buyers and tech executives are heating up the market and inflating house prices. I could not help but wonder if the family of Fu Liu bought an apartment here and whether it would be improper to ask him about it. I know the answer though. Nawin was so optimistic. If we leave, he said we could always rent it out and have that cover our mortgage. He said he did the costing and it made financial sense to buy. We compromised. I moved into his apartment in the Mission area and we agreed to spend one weekend a month looking for houses. I will keep you updated about any developments. Also, you need to visit us here soon. Kisses, L.

The Global Nomad Club
Suburban Living in the City: A reflection on urbanism in Manila
29 January 2014

Hey there, restless nomad hearts. It has been a few busy months—the same is apparently true for you. I am excited to say that our global nomad community has grown to over 4000! Thanks to everyone for sharing and posting—you are amazing!

My exciting news is that I moved in with my man—we shall call him N. Thanks to Andrea Roberts (andrearoberts_11) for reaching out and submitting her sharp observations on how expats shape the real estate market in Manila. It did make me think a lot about our decision (and financial ability) to buy a house, and if and how we contribute to changes in the city.

— ANDREA ROBERTS

"Suburban living in the city"—an advertisement for a new Ayala development in Manila offers. The slogan seems to be an oxymoron. Although technically what Ayala— a major real estate developer in the Philippines—is offering is feasible, who would want it? To whom is this development targeted?

Traditionally, people who choose to live in the suburbs do so in order to escape the city and its perceived ills such as crime, congestion and pollution. And those who actively choose to live in the city centre are unlikely to desire a suburban lifestyle or consider a move to the suburbs. They would be loath to give up the entertainment and cultural amenities of downtown living and to contend with a long commute to work and services.

Yet in Manila, this unlikely combination of urban and suburban is highly desired. The suburban lifestyle—with its shopping malls, car dependency and gated communities—is what the Ayalas and most developers are offering to their clients. The added bonus is that these suburban developments are located in the city centre, implying direct access to employment, services and amenities. In other words, you can have the suburban lifestyle without the commute. Manila developers are combining two distinct conditions— suburban and urban—into something intended to be better than the sum of its parts.

However, it seems to me that they are failing to realize the advantages of either urban or suburban. The idea that living in central Metro Manila avoids the trials and tribulations of a suburban commuter lifestyle is laughable for anyone who has experienced Manila's notorious traffic. And Manila offers few of the standard amenities you would expect to find in a metropolitan area of 12 million people. Few entertainment options exist outside of the malls. Now, before I am accused of overlooking the alternatives in the city, there are of course bars and restaurants and shops outside the malls, directly abutting the street. But the vast majority are located in malls, and most importantly, all new developments in the city are centred on a shopping mall. Office towers, residences, shops, restaurants and movie theatres are all developed by one company within one complex. For example, it would be possible to never leave the Greenbelt shopping centre in Makati if you lived in the Greenbelt Residences, worked in one of the office towers attached to the mall, and did all of your entertaining and shopping within the mall itself.

For those unfamiliar with Manila, this may seem like the ideal work-live-play development that is often encouraged in cities in developed countries. But the result is not what was intended by this theory of urban development. Anyone who has seen Greenbelt would not label it the pinnacle of smart development. On paper it sounds ideal but in actuality, it falls short of the work-live-play model. The idea behind work-live-play is to create vibrant neighbourhoods with all amenities and necessities on offer within walking distance or easily accessible by public transit. People therefore do not have to get in their cars to drive to the supermarket. Downtown business centres do not become deserted ghost towns at 5PM. The high density means that people interact with one another in their neighbourhood, on the streets, in the parks, all of which creates a vibrant community and dynamic streets. None of this is apparent in a standard Manila development.

Most standard Manila developments have a contrived feeling to them. Everything is overplanned; nothing has evolved organically. Each development is so similar to the next that it hardly matters which one you choose to visit. Even when you consider The Fort—a development that attempts to recreate the feel of a British high street—the result is much more similar to a traditional mall than anything found in a British town. It is difficult to pinpoint exactly why Manila's developments such as The Fort and Forbes Park feel oversanitized and do not achieve the dynamism they are aiming for. They have all the physical trappings of these idealized work-live-play developments or small towns, but they are missing a certain vitality and sense of community.

The standard answers come to mind as to why this is so: extreme inequality, endemic corruption, and security concerns. And these all do play a role. Extreme inequality means that few can afford to partake in the benefits of a new development. And even when those without are invited in, they are denied access. Guards prevent the son of a maid from using the swimming pool despite being accompanied by a resident. Maids and service workers must use different elevators from residents. High violent crime rates trump concerns with access. The poor are denied access to quasi-public spaces such as malls if they do not look wealthy enough to be a customer. It is assumed they will cause trouble, if not violence. What planning rules do exist are flaunted without penalty. But I think the root problems are whoever is doing the planning and whoever is the intended recipient of that planning.

In Manila, the main stakeholders doing the planning are developers. Now, of course, developers undertake site planning the world over. But in Manila, the scale at which developers plan and the lack of government or community oversight of that planning are what make this city different. Let's take the previously mentioned example of The Fort. Ayala Corporation and its partners have planned an area of 240 hectares.[5] Unlike in most cities, the developers own the entire plot, including the roads and access points. This means that all of the land, including the roads, sidewalks (where they exist), stores, condominiums, parks, and parking lots, are private. The result is that private guards regulate all car and foot traffic entering the complex and provide 24/7 surveillance of all the buildings and outdoor spaces. These guards are tasked with looking for security threats. Now this does include bombs and guns, but it also includes people who do not belong—those who are not wealthy enough to be customers or residents and those who do not have the correct employee security passes. Consequently, all undesirable elements—primarily the poor—can be removed from this private land without recourse. And of course, it is the landowner who determines who and what is undesirable.

This is the main method through which the developer creates and maintains the exclusivity of these developments. The slums come up to the invisible gates of *The Fort* but they come no further. There are no street vendors, no beggars, and no street performers. Absolutely nothing is happening on the streets or in the parks that is not sanctioned by the landowner and carefully marketed towards a small segment of society. Access points are carefully monitored throughout the day and most are closed off during the evening. Unlike most gated communities seen in the western world, *The Fort* does not have physical gates but its invisible barriers are no less keenly felt by those denied access. The result is a sterile, elitist environment.

In theory, the Metro Manila Development Authority (MMDA) is responsible for development planning in the fourteen constituent municipalities of the metropolitan area, but this authority rarely seems to be wielded to the benefit of the public. This, of course, depends on who your 'public' is. This brings us to the issue of who the developers —and by extension the MMDA—are planning for. The obvious answer is that they are planning for the small section of Manila society that includes wealthy Filipinos and expats—in other words, those who can afford to live in these suburban developments in the city.

So, despite their small numbers—likely numbering in the thousands in a metro region of at least 12 million people— Manila's expats have a disproportionately large impact on the development of their adopted city. Expats' demand for large, single-family housing in gated communities with exclusive amenities is shaping the growth of Manila. Yet expats are not the only group demanding this type of housing. Wealthy Filipino families are demanding similar types of developments. But unlike wealthy Filipinos, most expats would not be able to afford this lifestyle in their home countries. And many would not even want to live this type of lifestyle. When expats return home after a stint overseas, they do not look to recreate their expat lifestyle at home. Most Europeans, and even many North Americans, would never live in homes as big as the ones they choose to rent in Manila. It is neither possible financially nor culturally in their home countries. It is only when they go overseas that they begin to make such housing demands. Many expats would not normally think of spending all their leisure time walking around malls, shopping in malls, and eating in malls. But they choose to do so when they live in Manila.

This is partially because of the way many expat compensation packages are structured. Generous housing benefits allow expats to live a lifestyle that would be beyond their means at home. Embassies and multinational corporations tend to cover 100% of housing expenses up to a certain value, normally because it is expected that you have continuing housing expenses in your home country. International organizations, and some large not-for-profits, provide a housing allowance to cover up to 100% percentage of housing expenses. This is by no means abnormal for an expat package in Manila. Such generous housing benefits—which cannot be converted into another type of benefit—shape expats' housing choices.

Although this would not normally include housing benefits, many companies in North America are switching to a package of benefits model where staff can pick and choose from amongst a series of benefits based on their and their families' needs. Each staff is still provided the same remuneration through the benefits package but they can choose the specific benefits that are most appropriate for them based on their preferences. But in Manila, most embassies, multinational corporations, and development banks that hire expats do not take this modern approach. Staff must take the housing benefit as it is designed—even if it is not the most appropriate design for their needs—and cannot exchange it for another type of benefit. Some employers are changing their housing benefit structures by moving to a flat subsidy rather than a percentage, reducing the incentive to rent out-sized housing, but not eliminating it. The structure of housing benefit packages both incentivizes and allows expats to access a certain type of housing.

But it is not just a matter of incentives; it is also a matter of choice. I often heard expats say—and in fact, I often said myself—that they have to go to malls because there is nothing else and they have to be secure. Expats also say they have to demand this type of housing development for security reasons and to compensate for the difficulties of living in Manila. I was definitely guilty of this too. All this does is lead us to a circular argument. There are no other options because no one is demanding them. Mall-based developments continue to be built because people continue to go to them. Gated communities continue to be the gold standard because people choose to rent and buy in these communities. But if sales or attendance at the city's luxury malls declined, developers would take notice of this change in preference in shopping venue. If sales or leases within gated communities and luxury condominiums declined, developers would take notice of this change in preference in housing type.

I believe that many expats do not think they have any impact on their adopted city because they do not make up a large percentage of the city's residents. But through their influence and spending power, expats have a disproportionate impact on the urban environment. Through their housing and leisure choices, they can choose to make a positive impact on the future structure of Manila's urban development. Now, I am not saying that expats are not making a positive contribution to the life of the city in other ways. Most commonly, expat salaries for household staff tend to be noticeably higher than the average. And many expats volunteer their time and resources for charities and not-for-profits. Some even sponsor or foster orphaned children to ensure their needs are met, they are educated, and they have a chance at a better future. But in the realm of urban structure and inclusive urban development, most expats are not exercising the full potential of the positive impact they could have. Through more sensible housing and benefits packages, and a more deliberate consideration of how they exercise their housing and leisure choices, expats could have a lasting impact on the quality and structure of Manila's urban future.

Trace your steps, fellow nomad stars; Yours, lil_sea_girl

From: Leya.Nunez@gmail.com
To: Patricia.Nunez@gmail.com
Date: 17 May 2014. 22:59 adapt (San Francisco time)
Re: love&stars

My dear Patri, my letters to you have become much less frequent. I am not able to determine if this is a function of living away from home for so long or whether we just text and call more. But what I meant to be telling you for some time goes beyond the possibilities of a chat.

Nawin and I experienced so many misunderstandings lately. I don't know, we are just not in sync with ourselves and the larger universe. The other day I was late and so we missed the bus for our weekend trip. There and then I saw a new expression—a flicker of anger—on his face. I apologized and, unlike before, it took not minutes but hours to be comfortable and relaxed with each other again. The other night he reached out to hold me, but I had already turned away to pick up a book. A missed connection, happening so often lately. I saw him when I was sort of half-turned but I did not make the effort to turn back, nor did he try to reach out a second time. This may sound benign to you, but I just know we are changing.

Deep down I hear your smart voice, whispering that this might only be the passage from being in love to truly getting to know each other in a place where love merges with true friendship and becomes something else entirely. I am wondering, however, if love transforms through time similarly to the universe during its creation. The first nanoseconds of the universe meant immense pressure and heat causing particles to randomly move and crash into each other. The universe is still too hot and chaotic to create new permanent structures. With time-space expanding, the universe cools and allows particles to create stable elements through nuclear fusion. Hydrogen leads to more complex elements such as helium, lithium and beryllium. A hundred million years later, stars and galaxies form from these first elements. Stars are balanced by two opposite forces—gravity from their own mass, pulling the outer areas to the center, and the nuclear fusion of hydrogen on the inside of the star, which radiates energy and acts as counterpressure. Eventually, however, a star runs out of hydrogen, collapses under its own weight and dies, often accompanied by violent explosions or supernovas, emitting vast amounts of energy. The death of a star leaves its remaining center so hot and dense that it causes nuclear fusion reactions with surrounding gas and dust clouds, creating new and more complex elements such as oxygen and carbonate.

Maybe love is like the creation of its own universe and time-space. It starts from virtually nothing and then suddenly turns hot and dense, hormones flying through the brain and body, crashing into each other, bending reason and sometimes civility. With time, love—and the space it occupies—expands. And with expansion, love cools, becomes more stable and ultimately creates the most complex amalgamation of elements: new life. And just like for stars, opposite forces—attraction and fierce independence—create a fragile balance between lovers. When independence>attraction, and independence moves towards infinity, we collapse back into the singularity of ourselves. And while collapsing, translucent love wires, connecting two souls with their own time-space, burst and release energy of unpredictable intensity. Like then with Xavi. I can't live through this once again.

I want to bend the elements of the universe and find my way back to him. I want us so desperately to feel close again; like before, when our fingertips touched and I felt a direct lifeline to his heart. I wish we could have stayed hot, dark, and floating above the ground. But we have landed, for what it's worth. I wish you were here. I miss you so much. Love, L.

The Global Nomad Club
The Filipino diaspora—Portraits
23 May 2015

Hey there, restless hearts. Today I wanted to share a piece I started writing some time ago. Remember my trip to the Philippines? Thanks to conny11, I checked out this one shop at the Manila airport when I met a few women chatting and snacking while waiting for their flights. I told them about my dad, who left the Philippines to work as a seaman, found love and a family but not a home, and how I hoped I would not follow his exact footsteps. They also shared their stories, some of which were sad, while others were funny and hopeful. A few of them graciously agreed to be interviewed for this piece. I admired the courage of these women to travel to insecure destinations, where they work as maids, nannies and nurses, often fully depending on their employers. Their optimism and resilience made a lasting impression on me.

The Filipino diaspora—Portraits

"Globalization interconnected with a more general industrial restructuring has created service-based economies that are spatially concentrated in "global cities," the preferred production site of the post-industrial society. Empirical evidence suggests that the service sector creates occupational polarization by mainly creating jobs for the high- and low-skilled workers."[6]

"Manufacturing, that is in decline, used to decrease such polarization by requiring skilled labor. High unemployment, casualization and informalization of economic activities have decreased workers' bargaining power and have exacerbated income differentiation resulting from occupational polarization. Social polarization is an outcome of global city status and is not caused by globalization alone; empirical evidence suggests that social polarization results from a complex interaction between global, national, and local forces. Furthermore, albeit neglected in the literature, growth sectors in global cities attract (trans-) national labor migration that potentially aggravates social polarization by adding the highest and lowest skilled worker to the global city's workforce."[7] Up to date, the Philippines is one of the largest suppliers of labor to global cities. Approximately 10 million workers, or 10% of the population, are contributing to the wealth of other nations, sending home remittances to the extent of approximately 10% of GDP.

Myra: *Financing my children's education before returning home.* Myra lives in Riyadh, Saudi Arabia. She is the mother of two teenagers, a boy and a girl. She sees them once a year and is homesick most of the time. But her current work pays her five times more than what she would earn as a trained nurse in Manila. "Being a mother and working abroad, I can give my children the most I am able to give, despite the loneliness and being far away from them," Myra said. She is waiting for her elder son to finish university before returning home for good.

Candy: *A life I don't regret but don't wish on my daughter.* Candy lived in Singapore before returning to the Philippines with her daughter, who is now 6 years old. She initially left the Philippines because life was hard, and she wanted to see what else life could offer. While living in Singapore, she was able to visit her home in the Philippines only every 2 years. She sent her family her entire salary to finance her children's education. She does not regret her decision to work abroad but also says she would not want her children to live through what she did. She knows how hard and pressing life can be as an Overseas Filipino Worker (OFW). She would like to be involved with advocacy groups, creating jobs in the Philippines, but she has not come across such an initiative yet.

Beth: *I found good employment.* Beth has worked as a nanny in Dubai for more than 10 years. She was able to return every 2 years. She decided to leave the Philippines when she and her life partner broke up. She feels she is not treated badly and enjoys friends and food in her free time. Most of her income is sent back to her family. She does not feel homesick.

I am grateful to Myra, Candy and Beth for sharing their stories. Sleep tight, fellow nomad stars! Yours, lil_sea_girl.

From: Leya.Nunez@gmail.com
To: Patricia.Nunez@gmail.com
Date: 29 July 2015. 22:59 (San Francisco time)
Re: twitter

Dear Patri, how are you? I meant to write to you for some time. Nawin and I are in a better place. I feel even closer to him now that we have overcome this crisis. On a different note, I want professional change. I don't see myself in the e-commerce business in the long run. I met someone the other day from Twitter. They seem interested, not only in my previous experience, but also in my blog, and we are currently discussing an opening that might be a good fit for me. I will keep you posted. Talk soon, L.

The Global Nomad Club
Blast
16 November 2015

Hey there, restless nomad hearts. I was attending a friend's wedding when a blast hit first Beirut and the next day Paris. Everyone was on their phones checking in with friends and family, a sea of crossing messages and chat bubbles. "I am fine," "We were close," "This is the restaurant we used to go to," and finally, "marked safe." First there was sadness—everyone was reminded how brutally random death and tragedy can be—but after the first outrage (and everyone's loved ones were confirmed safe), we went back to celebrating life. Have we become cynical or just incredibly able to adapt to a different reality, one in which global terrorism has simply become part of our life? Sending thoughts and prayers to those affected.

Be safe, fellow nomad stars. Yours, lil_sea_girl.

Citizenship 2.0
29 June 2016

Hey there, restless nomad hearts. In the wake of Brexit, in which the United Kingdom narrowly decided to leave the European Union, I have reflected on multi-cultural societies and on the future of citizenship.

Citizenship 2.0

The concept of the nation-state is deeply rooted in our contemporary understanding of the world, and identity is often synonymous with nationality. The nation-state is commonly understood as "a sovereign state of which most of the citizens or subjects are united also by factors which define a nation, such as language or common descent."[8] But these identities have been challenged by globalization, turning nation-state identity into a more malleable concept. Societies today are looking ethnically more diverse than when nation-states started to emerge in the 19th century (many of these have however been preceded by multi-ethnic empires such as the Ottoman Empire or the Austro-Hungarian Empire). A legally codified citizenship and immigration system structures the belonging to contemporary nation-states: they are natives and naturalized citizens (full citizen), long-term residents (open-ended long-term residency permit), transitory migrants (with work permits and limited residency permits), refugees and illegal residents. Beyond these legal definitions, the cohesion of the urban social fabric in many societies revolves around the command of the same language of communication rather than a shared first (native) language, around common values and a shared understanding of rights and obligations rather than a unitary ethnicity and culture. Whereas Brexit revealed the discomfort multi-cultural societies generate with substantial part of the population, it equally demonstrates how they have become reality, irreversible only in scale, not in essence.

Beyond the contemporary reality of multi-cultural societies, transitory migrants or global nomads are at the forefront of challenging the current definition of citizenship by joining real and virtual communities of shared beliefs, experiences and values outside their home countries. They come to stay only a limited period of time, and do not necessarily seek full citizenship in the place of destination. Identifying as global nomads as well as a citizen from a specific nation-state, they embrace multiple identities.

Global nomads cross physical and virtual borders without the full control of the state (at least this is true for democracies). National authorities tend to carefully monitor the arrivals of foreigners at their borders. But at the same time, most democracies don't track their nationals leaving. Moving in and out of countries, they often evade the reach of tax authorities in the short term. In the medium term, they do join different aspects of the rights and obligations of citizenship, such as paying taxes or benefitting from public health schemes. But global nomads move to global cities not only for these tangible benefits and rights, but also for the opportunity to join a community of shared values. They enjoy the company of like-minded people sharing similar life experiences, with whom they have likely more in common than with many fellow citizens back in their home countries. A web-based platform called *InterNations* promises to connect expats. "Most of all, you want to meet others who understand your situation, who share your hobby and interests—other global minds, new friends...and with whom you share a certain view of the world—and probably an alma mater."

The Islamic State (IS) pushes the idea of a value-based citizenship even further by aspiring to create a transnational community of shared beliefs and values on a territory (within Syria and Iraq) with enforceable physical borders. Whereas the IS has not officially been recognized as a state, it carries out many of its functions. According to the Economist, the IS has established a basic taxation system based on an approximated 30% income tax rate. As much as 70% of its revenues is spent on military operations, and it is believed to have an estimated 80,000 fighters, including up to 30,000 foreign fighters. "Foreign fighters are particularly costly, with foreign Arabs being paid at least twice as much as locals, and European fighters getting over three times as much."[9] The IS has also started issuing birth certificates for newborns within their territory.

Its appeal is global, transcends ethno-nationalistic uniformity, and has attracted foreign fighters from an estimated 51 nations, using a narrative around exclusion, marginalization and humiliation of the Muslim community. Rebuilding bruised identities caused by economic and social exclusion, IS recruits are provided with a sense of belonging and purpose. The case of the IS is exemplary for the overlap of physical and virtual realms of global communities of values. Their active and professional use of social media to connect to other like-minded people has proven an incredibly successful strategy for recruitment. After having been actively recruited into the virtual IS community, they start planning to physically join them in Syria. The same applies to expats in global cities using social media and virtual networks to connect before, during and after their stay abroad. Overlapping physical and virtual networks transmit information and personal contacts to facilitate the process of leaving and integrating into a new society, as well as re-integrating back home.

Challenges to the traditional nation-state also come from a different group. Digital nomads, around the group of cyber-punks of Satoshi Nakamuro, created virtual currencies as a way to depend less on state authority in the aftermath of the global economic crisis, which has highlighted the challenges of the state-centric international financial system to maintain financial stability. Virtual currencies, such as bitcoin, are based on ledger-distributed technology on the blockchain. Permissionless systems do not require a central authority, because the trust lies with the inherent governance structure using a verifiable algorithm to confirm the validity of transactions. The currency theoretically has the potential to become the currency of the global nomad tribe —if accepted at sufficient pay-points in the future. It transcends physical borders and state control, is transnational by definition, and inclusive to everyone with a computer. Currently, however, their wider use is premature because they are too volatile, riddled with security breaches and misused for criminal activities.

Governments around the world react to global nomads challenging the notion of a fixed and linear understanding of citizenship. Canada set an interesting precedent by temporarily revoking voting rights for their citizen living abroad but reversed its decision after extensive protests. It just highlights that citizenship is not fixed but stretchable, transformable especially over time. The UK has decided to grant EU citizens the right to vote at the communal level (these will however be reversed after Brexit). France and UK announced plans to revoke citizenship of their nationals joining IS. Another example is Saudi Arabia, which recently granted citizenship to a female robot. "Estonia has also pioneered the concept of e-residency as a form of transnational digital identity. It is available to anyone in the world interested in using Estonian online services, open a bank account, or start a company. E-residents can apply for a bank account, conduct online banking, declare taxes, sign documents remotely, and get access to international payment providers."[10]

In light of all these developments, do you think identifying as a global nomad is a political act or a purely personal quest? Will nation-states eventually morph into social contracts based on common experiences and values—in overlapping physical and virtual realms—transcending traditional notions of citizenship rooted in irreversibility, ethnicity, and defined space? Would it be preceded by civil war and the dissolution of existing nation-states? Is choosing a community of values the ultimate expression of the enlightenment ideals of reason, free choice and a truly global sorority? A world in which experiences, values and beliefs shape and determine citizenship—would it eventually bring more peace and political stability or create homogenous value spaces void of innovation and progress?

Sleep tight, fellow nomad stars. Yours, lil_sea_girl.

From: Leya.Nunez@gmail.com
To: Patricia.Nunez@gmail.com
Date: 24 July 2016. 22:57 (San Francisco time)
Re: peace

My Patri, Nawin and I are still us, and I must admit there are days that I am still surprised. I guess deep down I still expect for everything to fall apart, like the time with Xavi. Though my heart and mind have healed, my body still remembers. There are days when I take a step and suddenly the pain resurfaces, paralyzes me for a fraction of a second and then quickly disappears into my subconscious again. On these days, I rush home from work to be with Nawin and find him quietly planting tomatoes, zucchinis and kale on our rooftop, his shoulders and entire body tense and dedicated to every task at hand. I love him for it. You know how much I hate gardening—it does not relax me at all—but ironically it gives me peace to watch Nawin attend to the plants with the kind of care and patience that is alien to me.

On a different note, we've started regularly rock-climbing with a group of friends. I am shocked that I am physically able to do so after all those years of partying and drinking. Last weekend, we went to Yosemite. While climbing the Nutcracker, my forearms got totally pumped and I ended up dropping my quickdraws. I was in big trouble; unable to finish the route, but without enough rope to rappel down. Priya, a friend visiting from Melbourne, saw that I was in distress and came to help me finish the route. You know how much I dislike being helped in front of other people. Maybe it was the serenity of our surroundings or the quiet manner in which she offered her hand, but I was just glad she did.

When I was waiting for Nawin to ascend, I started thinking about Abuela. And then, out of nowhere, I thought about Abuelo before Franco, before they came for him in the middle of the night and arrested him for being a socialist. How he disappeared that night and that we never got to meet him. I imagined him being shot and I always wondered about his last thoughts—they must have been about Abuela and Maman. In my nightmares, I dreamt about his body in a mass grave with so many others. I thought about Abuela before she began wearing her long dress of mourning. I pictured them holding hands and walking through the local pine forests. I don't think I've ever seen her as happy as in my dream. Maybe it was her birthday and he surprised her with a picnic. I could smell the pines. I felt the softness of grass and pine needles under her feet. I heard the hum of the world muffled through the trees. The breeze softly played with her light, yellow linen dress, which caressed her legs with every step. It was such a peaceful thought. Maybe I couldn't envision her happy before because I had not been happy myself. I think about whether her health would allow her to visit San Francisco. Would she accept her granddaughter from the sea if she saw her relaxed and walking in the pines around here? I thought about our house in Barcelona and its inflexible foundation. Rather than frighten and suffocate me like it usually did, I envisioned myself using its spine to lift myself up to the roof of our house where I sat quietly, observing people and houses from above.

When Nawin finally reached the top, he immediately saw that my mind was far away and for once did not ask any questions. He simply smiled and held me for a long time. When we were back in the car, I felt like telling him about my special moment but decided to keep it to myself, just in case he could not fully fathom my happiness or its meaning. I would have been disappointed in him. I preferred to believe that deep down he understood. Instead, I went on about my work and how I hoped to finish certain projects over the coming months. I teased him about the upcoming primaries. I want Hillary to win while he feels strongly for Senator Bernie Sanders. I said she is unfairly criticized for being a strong, driven woman, qualified and ambitious enough to run for president. He disagrees, and points out how the Clintons have supported laws leading to mass incarcerations. "You don't have the experience of living as a black man in the US," he snaps at me. "So you think she is responsible for the policies of her husband?" I shoot back. We debate the entire drive back home. Much love, L.

The Global Nomad Club
Migrating humans
31 August 2016

Hey there, restless hearts. I hope you are doing all right. Over the last months I have been trying to digest the images of refugees flowing into Europe to escape the horrors of civil conflict and terrorism in Syria, Iraq and Afghanistan. The TV host says 65 million people are on the run—the largest migration crisis since the Second World War.

Migrating humans

Societies contemplate on how many refugees to accept. Three and a half million refugees found shelter in Turkey. One million arrived in Germany. People are waiting at the train station to receive them. Most towns and cities are touched by the newly arrived. There is hatred. And fear. I wonder, what came first? There are concerns. Can they be integrated? What about women's rights? How will the education system deal with the influx of kids who do not speak the local language yet? Volunteers collect clothes and musical instruments—after all, they came with almost nothing. People complain about them owning cellphones as if having them means they do not need our help. A drowned boy—Aylan Kurdi—at the beach provokes bubbled compassion and then the return to normalcy.

A bright, young refugee from Iraq shared a personal message through my blog. "Germany is not yet home, but still the closest I have to a home. Do you understand that I never wanted to leave Iraq—I mean before the war? But Iraq no longer qualifies as home—everyone I knew is either dead or has left the country. Now, I want to stay in Germany and study computer science." Her immigration status is still uncertain, as her hometown is considered safe again. I pray that she will be able to keep her imperfect new home.

The newspapers tell stories about heroines, personal tragedies and the cities they left behind bombed to rubble. Migrating humans are a business, say the smugglers. The laws of demand and supply equally applies to human misery. The United Nations declares a record number of refugees—5000 to be precise—drowned in the Mediterranean this year. There are more stories, more facts, but the truth is best expressed in poems. Have you read them?

Our experience is different. I re-rooted myself multiple times voluntarily—and have often been received enthusiastically. You did not choose to squash your life into a tiny bag. You only chose when to leave. Taking the boat was not your choice either—you prefer driving. Rejected countless times by countries, borders and people throughout the journey, until it is hard to still feel human.

In some small ways, though, I understand what you are saying. A physical connection to the earth we walked since childhood provides certainty and a firm step. The relation to the sun and trees we are from is not neutral. And after leaving the sun and trees behind, an endless flow of people and new connections awaits. First there are too many to remember. Then comes the realization that most encounters can be summed up into two categories: the kind ones and the less kind ones. Perhaps you did not notice this pattern before, but then you never depended on someone else's kindness as much as you do now.

And what happens exactly at the intersection of residents and migrants colliding? Can we truly understand each other, or are we by definition alone in our most existential moments? How to translate fear into effective language? How to express that her certitude is your only desire, when she is sitting at her dinner table dreaming of a new beginning? Envy often goes both ways.

How to rebuild a life when you have forgotten how to dream? During the entire journey, the body and brain have been squeezed for a last step, and then another. Recovery starts when the muscles are allowed to breathe again. But the brain—how to make the brain stop hurting? Complete exhaustion becomes an everyday companion while walking those long new streets. People, so certain of their direction, pass by and realize that your walk is a bit hesitant, but they are unable to apprehend the reasons within.

One random day, time for grieving home and loved ones is up, and you are asked to rejoin the world of happy and productive people. But they don't realize that there is a dark place after grief and loss have become bearable. It is precisely then that life's meaning has to be carefully recreated piece by piece—a challenging call on the human condition under every circumstance. I just now remember a few lines of the short story I read many years ago: "Everyone comes with a unique story worth listening to. I hope you will."

I root for more connections. The kind ones. Yours, lil_sea_girl.

From: Leya.Nunez@gmail.com
To: Patricia.Nunez@gmail.com
Date: 29 October 2016. 22:59 (San Francisco time)
Re:

Patri, it was wonderful to have you here again. I wish you could have stayed longer. I am happy we found the time to speak about Dad. After all these years, I truly feel like his daughter, embracing this quest for adventure he instilled in my heart. But unlike him, I found balance and a true home in Nawin. And if I leave San Francisco, it will be with him. I love you so much, L.

From: Leya.Nunez@gmail.com
To: Patricia.Nunez@gmail.com
Date: 9 November 2016. 22:59 (San Francisco time)
Re: post-election

Dear Patri, I am terrified. There are rumors of foreign influence and manipulation in the presidential election. The strongest country on earth swayed by internet bots directed through foreign agents. Language of hate, racism, and sexism have become more prevalent and visible. We live in different times. I feel personally affected. Will I be able to renew my visa? Will I be grabbed—well, because they can? Life suddenly feels less stable, less secure. It is said that voters did reject globalization. To me, globalization seemed like an irreversible historical process, but then history might be less linear than I previously assumed. Maybe this is nothing more than a short reversal—a reminder to more actively shape the process of globalization and give it a more human face. I feel sad and somewhat speechless. Yours, L.

The Global Nomad Club
Ode
14 April 2017

Hey there, restless hearts. I have not fully adjusted to the new normal, but I had ample time to reflect on recent political events. And after being depressed for several months, I have started to appreciate the opportunities to sharpen and re-define the liberal progressive movement in its brush with the nationalist ideology of the current political sentiment on both sides of the Atlantic. Do you think it is a coincidence that the most important contemporary social reckoning of the women's rights movements (#metoo) started under a president set to win voters by proudly owning and displaying the ugliness of patriarchy? Young climate activists are organizing protests against climate change and for a future on our planet. It is with this knowledge that I am able to contemplate other important questions in life.

I sit outside, the heart filled with light as a half-moon extends over a silver-dipped bay. My thoughts drift off to past cities and friends I made along the way. I sense a craving sending neurotransmitters in the brain to spin, and a sudden inkling. I look at N and wonder if another destination calls us. Tomorrow will know the answer. Or the day after tomorrow. For tonight, my home is the sea and his heartbeat quietly syncing with mine.

I feel the circumference of my soul softening to connect with the inaudible rhythm of the universe, and through it to all of your stories in these eternal stretches of time and failing stars. Your voices enlarge my world—thank you! In sharing our adventures, our questions and those moments of loneliness, we have become of each other. More than a club, I consider us a fragmented but connected global community. United above all in the quest for reckoning with continuous re-positioning in space and the re-purposing of life that follows: a search for splendor in its own right. Oh, then—Restless Nomad Heart—leave and grow much stronger![11]

Stay up with me tonight, fellow nomad stars! Sincerely yours, Leya.

THE END

EPILOGUE

I was about to publish the book when the Corona virus put the world on lockdown. Writing this book would not be complete without a view on how this virus may shape globalization. The response to the Corona pandemic taught us that globalization is not a deterministic process, and that indeed the world can stop flying. Will the crisis bring de-globalization, i.e. closed borders, the nationalization of supply chains for essential goods, and the breakdown of global cooperation? Or will it bring back a renewed under-standing that globally coordinated responses are the only solution for our connected world? A new Cold War or increased collaboration to fight the global climate crisis?

Along similar lines, I wonder how the climate change crisis will affect globalization. Inspired by young climate change activists, a global movement has organized protests demanding policy makers and companies to act before it is too late. These young activists vow not to fly and make fewer physical connections, but they do connect and organize globally through the internet.

And then George Floyd—murdered by police while the world was watching. A powerful reminder that we not only face different realities when crossing borders, but also within them. And while social change remains painfully slow, the protests in the US immediately spread to societies all over the world. After expressing solidarity with the Black Lives Matter movement on social media, a local bar in Berne was challenged to change its name—Colonial Bar— overnight and is called Versa now. On the other side of the world, K-Pop fans diluted racist hashtags in solidarity with what is happening in the United States. The world is chang- ing, one global conversation at a time.

Even if the world is under lockdown, flies less and redesigns supply lines, we remain connected as we begin to under- stand that we are a fragile component of a much larger ecosystem. The pandemic taught us that we can approach life differently. It also means that we can and must shape globalization for the better.

The Global Nomad Club
New beginnings
31 January 2021

Hey there, restless nomad hearts, how are you holding up? I am writing to you from my hotel room in Washington DC. Arrived from Ghana, I have to self-quarantine. I am here to support the incoming administration on data governance and social media. Data is the new oil, golden, but so extrac- tive. What should be the rules of engagement?

Sorry—N is waking up, so my time to write to you is up. Thank you again for your loyalty; TikTok is just not my thing. Stay healthy, fellow nomad stars, and above all keep happy in these most unusual times! Still yours, Leya

ABOUT THE AUTHOR

I spent more than a decade exploring the world. First, as a student in Madrid, Bangkok and London, and later, as a project manager for development projects in Shanghai, Yaoundé and Manila. Today, I live in Switzerland with my husband and young son.

The *Global Nomad Club* is a collaboration with the following contributing authors:

Glimpes (Reprint[1]) - Pooya Ghoddousi
Under my Skin - Scott Burroughs
Urban Nomad: a Brand in Motion - Jepkemoi
My Eid-al-Fitr in Mindanao - Gabriela Blatter
To live where Life is precarious - Stefan Bigler
Good bye and Arrivederci - Yours faithfully, the young - Ruben Barreto
Global City Magnet - Maciej Bugala
Suburban living in the City: a reflection on Urbanism in Manila - Andrea Roberts
The Filipino Diaspora - Portraits - Candy Estolatan, Beth Cabagon and Myra Ferrer

The book has been published with the generous contribution of the the *Global Nomad Publishers*:

Tobias Engelmeier
Tatjana Lanaras (continued)

Sponsor from India
Carlo Bertsch
Cédric Crelo
Rolf Dieter Beck
Vivan Sharan
Sponser from Norway
Fan of Theodor Heuss
Silent Supporter
Juliette Leusink
Jana Wettich
Mimi Bertsch-Jabas
Anjali Gill
Monika Sommer
Frauke Bohn
Simone Lerch
Silent supporter
Florina Tarasov
Silent supporter
Sheilani Alix
Gaby
Hartmut Riedel
Silent supporter
Jasminka Kumbric
Lara Born
Maurice Lindgren
Ana Maria Torres
Seline Iseli
Shahbano Tirmizi
AFGG friend
Irene Frei
Valentina Barcucci
Ivana Igic

NOTES

Chapter 1

1. Perhaps the main reason for the nomads to look down upon gypsies was their feeling of higher status due to their productiveness and the resultant independence and pride.
2. Over the past 15 years, the number of people crossing borders in search of a better life has been rising steadily. At the start of the 21st century, one in every 35 people is an international immigrant. If they all lived in the same place, it would be the world's fifth-largest country. (BBC NEWS, migration factfile, June 2004).
3. Iranians are among the most visible nationalities in e-communities and internet friends networks (i.e. third in 'Orkut' and growing in 'Gazzag').
4. Toby Berger Holtz. The Hall Family and Ethiopia: A Century of Involvement.

Chapter 2

1. https://www.bbc.co.uk/science/horizon/2001/paralleluni.shtml

Chapter 3

1. Dr. Thomas Köllen, Arbeitssituation and Arbeitsklima für Deutsche in der Schweiz. Wirtschaftsunviversität Wien. 2015

Chapter 4

1. Hermann Hesse (Stufen)
2. OECD. 2005. *Counting Immigrants and Expatriates in OECD Countries: A New Perspective*. Paris.
3. www.swissinfo.ch (accessed on 23 January 2014).
4. Eurostat. http://epp.eurostat.ec.europa.eu (accessed on 23 September 2014).
5. www.fbdcorp.com

6. Natalie Bertsch. Master thesis (quoting Saskia Sassen—the global city). LSE

7. Natalie Bertsch. Master thesis (quoting Saskia Sassen—the global city). LSE

8. https://en.wikipedia.org/wiki/Nation_state#:~:text=According%20to%20one%20definition%2C%20%22a,have%20a%20predominant%20ethnic%20group.

9. https://www.economist.com/middle-east-and-africa/2015/12/12/degraded-not-yet-destroyed

10. World Bank. Distributed Ledger Technology (DLT) and blockchain. 2017

11. Herman Hesse, Stufen, rephrased

About the Author

1. The essay was first published in Letters from Tentland by Susanne Vincenz (Trancript Verlag. 2005)

www.ingramcontent.com/pod-product-compliance
Lightning Source LLC
LaVergne TN
LVHW031238190726
843491LV00012B/3045